ENGLISH-LANGUAGE LEARNERS

STUDENT HANDBOOK

www.harcourtschool.com

Printed in the United States of America

ISBN 10 0-15-367057-6

ISBN 13 978-0-15-367057-2

2 3 4 5 6 7 8 9 10 197 16 15 14 13 12 11 10 09 08 07

CONTENTS

CONTENTS

Language-Learning Strategy

Use What You Know

You can use what you know to help you understand what you read.

Bonsai trees are like regular trees, but they grow no higher than a person's knee. To make a bonsai, a gardener puts a young tree in a very small container instead of in the ground. In the container, the bonsai's roots can't grow very far. The gardener also can control the size of the tree by cutting back the roots.

- **Use prior knowledge**
  "A bonsai tree must look like a regular tree, only smaller."
- **Think about expressions**
  "I think *no higher* means the same as *no taller*."
- **Reason**
  "A bonsai tree can be as beautiful as a regular tree and take up less space."

Language-Learning Strategy

Find Help

If you need help understanding what you read, look around you.

Mammoth Cave National Park in Kentucky has the longest known cave system in the world. It is about 348 miles long and 379 feet deep. There are more than seventy threatened or endangered species living in the park. Many of these plants and animals could not live in other places because they have adapted to life in a cave environment."

- **Use a computer**
  "I can look for a map of Kentucky on the Internet."

- **Ask for help**
  "I can ask my teacher or a friend how to say *species*."

- **Use books**
  "The dictionary says that to adapt is to change because of conditions."

Make Connections

Try to make connections between what you read and your own experience.

Antarctica is an interesting place to study because of its very cold climate. Scientists have discovered that fish can survive in Antarctica's icy waters because their blood contains a kind of antifreeze. On the surface of Antarctica, scientists have found thousands of rocks from outer space. Scientists also have discovered that several lakes lie beneath Antarctica.

- **Use word structure**
  "The prefix *anti-* means the same as *not*. Antifreeze must be something that does not freeze."

- **Compare and contrast**
  "Antarctica is mostly cold and snowy, but Florida is sunny and warm."

- **Use maps and charts**
  "Antarctica covers the South Pole. Maybe that is why it's so cold."

Language-Learning Strategy

Picture It

Making pictures in your mind can help you understand.

Every summer my younger sister and I visit our grandparents in Colorado. They have a small farm, and we help them with the chores while we're there. Every morning it's my job to feed the animals and to gather eggs for breakfast. My sister and I also groom and exercise our grandparent's horses. Taking care of the horses is our favorite chore.

- **Describe it**
  "To help me remember the events, I describe the chores to a classmate."
- **Memorize**
  "I pick out important words that describe the subject. Then I create a word web to help me remember them."
- **Use actions**
  "I think about how the children would complete their chores. I act out how I think they would do them."

Language-Learning Strategy

Look for Patterns

Looking for words and word parts that are the same can help you understand what you read.

If all the seas were one sea,
What a *great* sea that would be!
If all the trees were one tree,
What a *great* tree that would be!
And if all the axes were one axe,
What a *great* axe that would be!
And if all the men were one man,
What a *great* man that would be!
And if the *great* man took the *great* axe,
And cut down the *great* tree,
And let it fall into the *great* sea,
What a splish-splash that would be!

- **Use repetition**
  Lines 2, 4, 6, and 8 have a pattern.
- **Think about words and phrases**
  "I think *splish-splash* tells me the sound that the sea makes when the tree falls in."
- **Use text structure**
  The first eight lines include *sea*, *tree*, *axe*, and *man*. The last four lines repeat those words, but in reverse order.

Language-Learning Strategy

Set a Purpose

Think about what you want to learn or tell.

Paper products, glass bottles, plastic bags, and aluminum can are all items that can be recycled. By recycling, you can conserve natural resources and preserve the Earth for people in the future. Recycling also saves money for both you and your city.

- **Purpose for listening**
  "I will listen to find out what I can recycle."
- **Purpose for speaking**
  "I want to talk with my classmates about starting a recycling program at our school."
- **Purpose for reading**
  "I want to find out why people should recycle."
- **Purpose for writing**
  "I want to write a report about the materials than can be recycled."

Lesson 1

Background and Vocabulary

Selections You Will Read

- "Rope Burn"
- "Tree Houses for Everyone"

"Rope Burn" is **realistic fiction**. Realistic fiction

- has characters who have feelings that real people have
- has a main character who overcomes a challenge

What is "Rope Burn" about?

This selection is about a boy, Richard, who is trying to fit in at his new school. Richard learns to overcome an obstacle with the help of a new friend.

Overcoming an obstacle means to deal with something that is preventing you from doing what you would like to do.

This person is overcoming the obstacle of being in a wheelchair. ▶

What vocabulary will you learn?

Robust Vocabulary

- humiliation
- expectations
- fringes
- hesitating
- sincere
- coaxed

Tip

Remember to look in the glossary for explanations of the words. What other strategies can you use?

Word Bank

Comprehension

What is the focus skill in this lesson?

The focus skill is **Plot: Conflict and Resolution.**

Fiction stories have a plot.

Conflict is a problem or challenge.

Resolution is how the problem is solved.

The **plot** is the events, or what happens, in a story. In most plots, the main character has a **conflict**, or problem. The plot tells how the conflict is **resolved**, or solved.

Read the passage

Jill's family moved from America to France. Jill could not speak French very well. At school she was very lonely. One day, a girl named Anne came up to her. Anne had an idea. They could practice speaking with each other. Anne could teach Jill French, and Jill could teach Anne English. Jill liked that idea.

The plot tells of a girl that moves to France and how she makes a new friend. The conflict is that Jill cannot speak French and is lonely. The resolution is that Jill meets a new friend who will teach her French.

Grammar and Writing

What kind of writing will you do in this lesson?

You will write a **character description**. You will use a personal voice to write a character description. Here is a short character description:

This describes what the character looks like.

James loves to run. He runs all the time. James is a tall, thin boy with curly hair that bounces when he runs. He is the fastest boy in our grade. James always looks happy when he is running.

What is the grammar skill?

You will learn about **complete sentences**.
A complete sentence has a **subject** and a **verb**.

James runs to school.

Decoding–Spelling Connection

The short /e/ vowel sound can be spelled *e* or *ea*.

chest	**measure**
chest	mea sure

You can keep things in a chest.

Lesson 2

Background and Vocabulary

Selections You Will Read

- "Line Drive"
- "Ninth Inning"

"Line Drive" is an **autobiography**. An **Autobiography**

- is a person's account, or story, of his or her own life
- is written in the first-person point of view
- gives details about important events in the author's life

What is "Line Drive" about?

Tanya West Dean writes about growing up in the 1960s when she dreamed of playing baseball with the boys. In the 1960s, girls were not allowed to play on boys' teams. Tanya had to overcome discrimination in order to play with the boys.

Discrimination means unfair behavior to others based on differences. These differences can include race, age, religion, and whether someone is male or female.

In the early 1900s, women were not allowed to vote. This was discrimination.

What vocabulary will you learn?

Robust Vocabulary

- maven
- reigned
- designated
- exhilarated
- mortified
- conceited
- smirk

Tip

Remember to look in the Glossary for explanations of the words. What other strategies can you use?

Word Bank

scorekeeper

bleachers

pitcher

batter

Comprehension

What is the focus skill in this lesson?

The focus skill is **Plot: Conflict and Resolution**

Autobiographical stories have a **plot**.

Conflict is a problem or challenge.

Resolution is how the problem is solved.

The plot is the events, or what happens, in a story. In most plots, the main character has a **conflict**, or problem. The plot tells how the conflict is **resolved**, or solved.

Read the passage.

The kids in the neighborhood were playing soccer. Nobody wanted Alma on his or her team. Alma was the smallest girl in the fifth grade. Nobody thought she would be a good player. Finally the kids agreed to give her a chance. Alma got the ball. She ran past the other players and kicked the ball into the goal. Then one of the kids said, "Wow! I want Alma on my team."

The conflict is that Alma wants to play soccer, but the other kids think she is too small. The plot action is that Alma makes a goal and proves she is a good player. The resolution is that that Alma is asked to be on one of the teams.

Grammar and Writing

What kind of writing will you do in this lesson?

You will write an **autobiographical composition**. You will use your own voice when writing your composition. Here is a short autobiographical composition:

I've been drumming on things for as long as I can remember. When I was little, I drummed on pots and pans. Then my parents bought me real drums. I'm the smallest girl in my class, but I can make big sounds come out of those drums. Most people think those sounds are pretty good.

Tells what the author looks like

Tells about the author's abilities

What is the grammar skill?

You will learn about **imperative sentences**, **exclamatory sentences,** and **interjections**.

Throw the ball over here. — imperative sentence

Wow! This game is exciting! — exclamatory sentence

Decoding–Spelling Connection

The long *a* sound can be spelled different ways.

obtain		**saying**	
ob	**tain**	**say**	**ing**

This girl is saying something.

Lesson 3

Background and Vocabulary

Selections You Will Read

- "Chang and the Bamboo Flute"
- "Evren Ozan, Musician"

"Chang and the Bamboo Flute" is **historical fiction**. Historical fiction

- is about people, places, and events from the past
- has characters who have feelings that real people have
- gives details that help the reader picture the setting

What is "Chang and the Bamboo Flute" about?

This selection is about a boy, Chang, who tries to sell his most important possession in order to help his family. However, Chang learns that his own talents are his most important possession.

A **talent** is a special skill or ability.

What vocabulary will you learn?

Robust Vocabulary

- pried
- desperately
- sneered
- indignantly
- urgently
- grudgingly

Tip

Remember to look in the Glossary for explanations of the words. What other strategies can you use?

Word Bank

Comprehension

What is the focus skill in this lesson?

The focus skill is **Character's Motives.**

Historical fiction has characters with motives.

A **motive** is a reason for doing something or behaving in a certain way.

Authors reveal, or show, a **character's motives** by describing the character's thoughts, actions, and words.

Read the passage.

Leah looked at the sign for the dance contest. The winner would get $100. Leah was a good dancer, but she did not like to dance in front of strangers. Leah started to walk away, but then she thought about her mother. Winter was coming, and her mother wanted a new coat. Leah decided to enter the contest. She knew what she would buy if she won the contest.

Leah's motive for entering the dance contest is to buy her mother a new coat.

Grammar and Writing

What kind of writing will you do in this lesson?

You will write an **Autobiographical Narrative**. This is a story you write about yourself. You will choose vivid words that clearly tell your ideas and create a picture in the reader's mind. Here is a short autobiographical narrative:

This gives the setting.

This is a vivid word.

These words clearly tell an idea.

I stood on the diving board at the swimming pool. The other kids in the pool were laughing and splashing each other. I wish I felt like them, but I didn't. I felt scared. The water below looked very far away. But I had promised myself that this year I would learn how to dive.

What is the grammar skill?

You will learn about **subjects** and **predicates**.

Decoding–Spelling Connection

The /ow/ sound can be spelled *ou* or *ow*.

counter		powder	
coun	ter	pow	der

A counter is a long, flat surface. You can put things on a counter.

Lesson 4

Background and Vocabulary

Selections You Will Read

- "The Daring Nellie Bly: America's Star Reporter"
- "Around The World In Seventy-two Days"

"The Daring Nellie Bly: America's Star Reporter" is a **biography**. A **biography**

- is a written account of a person's life, told by someone else
- often presents events in time order
- gives information that shows why the person's life is important

What "The Daring Nellie Bly: America's Star Reporter" about?

This selection is about an American reporter named Nellie Bly. Nellie Bly wanted to travel around the world in less than eighty days. She faced many difficulties, but she showed great perseverance in reaching her goal.

Perseverance means continuing to try hard, even when you face obstacles or delays. When you persevere, you make your best effort.

This runner is tired, but she is still trying to finish.

What vocabulary will you learn?

Robust Vocabulary

- relented
- faze
- eccentric
- infuriated
- disheartened
- impassable
- crusaded

Tip

As you learn new words, remember to write them in your Vocabulary Log. Which words do you know very well? Which words are you still learning?

Word Bank

newspaper

luggage

fireworks

pier

Comprehension

What is the focus skill in this lesson?

The focus skill is **Character's Motives.**

Biographies have characters with motives.

A **motive** is a reason for doing something or behaving in a certain way

Authors reveal, or show, a character's motives by describing the character's thoughts, actions, and words.

Read the Passage.

The year was 1846. Mary waited to get on the ship that would take her and her family to America. It would be a hard journey, but Mary knew she could not stay in Ireland. A disease had killed all the crops. There was nothing to eat and there were no jobs. Mary knew she could find work in America. As Mary waited, she thought, "In America, my family will have a better life."

Mary's thoughts show her motive for going to America. She is taking her family to America to give them a better life.

Grammar and Writing

What kind of writing will you do in this lesson?

You will write a **newspaper story**. You will choose vivid words and phrases that clearly tell your ideas and create a picture in the reader's mind. Here is a short newspaper story:

This tells **what** the story is about and **when** it took place.

This is a vivid phrase.

A large storm hit our city yesterday morning. By 6:00 A.M., the sky was full of thick, black clouds. Soon, the rain poured down, and strong winds began to blow. By noon, three trees had been knocked over by the winds. People were told to stay indoors until the storm had passed..

What is the grammar skill?

You will learn about **complete** and **simple subjects** and **predicates**.

The hungry boy ate a lot of pizza.

complete predicate

complete subject

simple subject

simple predicate

Decoding–Spelling Connection

When the root word ends with a silent *e*, drop the e before adding *-ing*.

smiling		changing	
smil	ing	chang	ing

This child is smiling.

Lesson 5

Review

Background and Vocabulary

Selections You Will Read

You will read a selection titled "It Takes Talent!" The selection is a **Readers' Theater**.

READERS' THEATER

You will also read a story titled "The Alligator Race." This selection is **realistic fiction**. Realistic fiction tells about characters and events that could happen in real life.

COMPREHENSION STRATEGIES

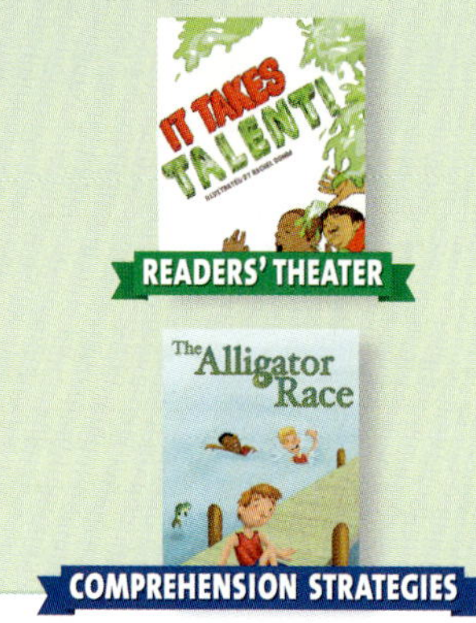

What are the selections about?

"**It Takes Talent!**" is about a boy who doesn't know how he will participate in a talent show. To his surprise, he ends up making the talent show a big success.

"**The Alligator Race**" is about a boy, Steve, who has joined a water-sports team. Steve is afraid of swimming in the lake. Steve's teammates help him to face his fear.

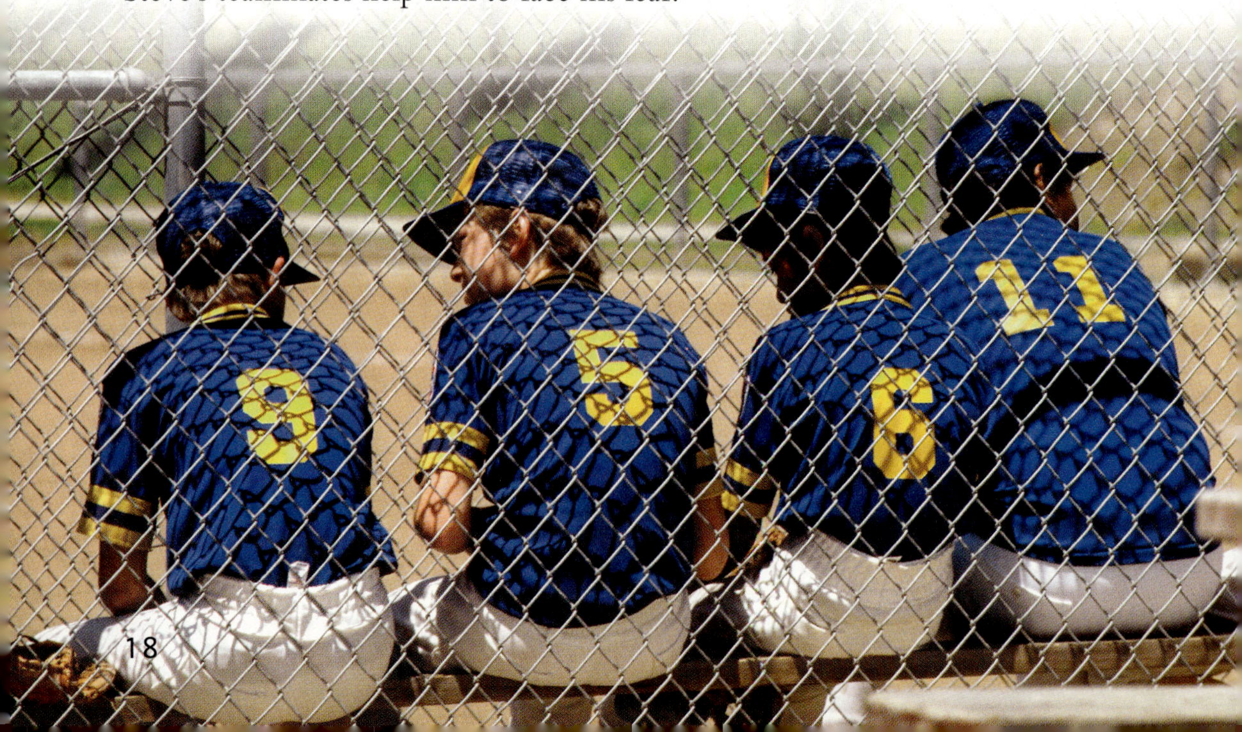

What vocabulary will you learn?

Robust Vocabulary

- genial
- prognostication
- stricken
- dramatically
- restrain
- protest
- feverishly
- overcome
- flop
- spectacular

Remember to look in the Glossary for explanations of the words. What other strategies can you use?

Word Bank

freckles

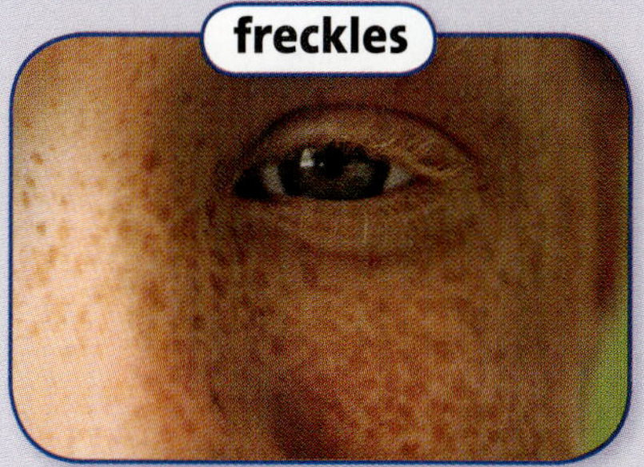

alligator

ballet

carton

gelatin

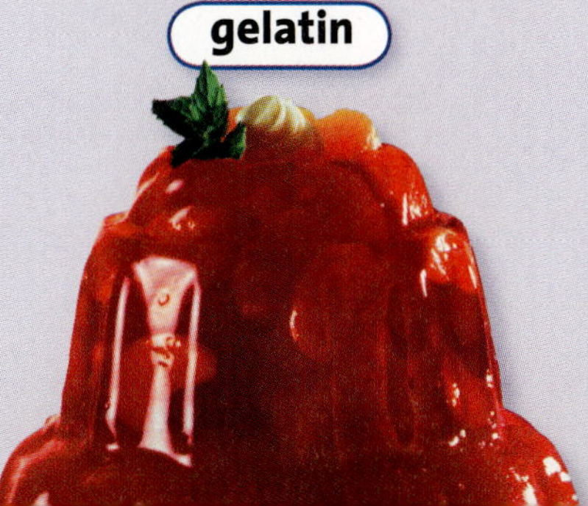

Fluency

As you read "It Takes Talent!" you will build fluency. When you read a script aloud, remember to

- read with **accuracy**
- use appropriate **reading rate** to help you and your listeners understand your lines

Comprehension Strategies

As you read "The Alligator Race," you will review the two comprehension strategies you learned in Theme 1.

- **Use Story Structure** As you read, think about the characters, setting, and plot events of the story. Identify the problem the main character needs to solve and how it is resolved.
- **Monitor Comprehension: Reread** If you don't understand something, reread it for clarification.

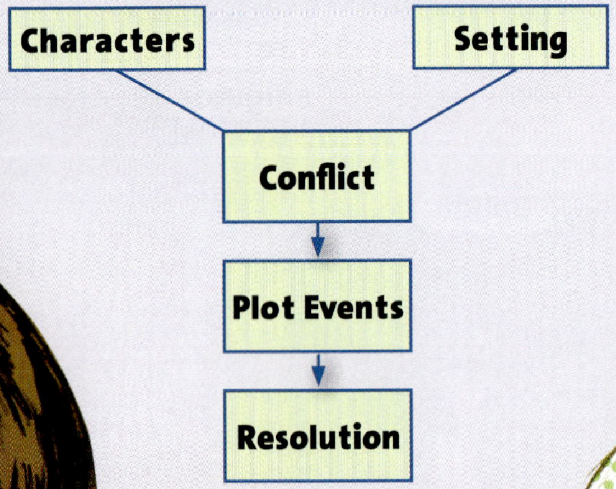

Characters
Setting
Conflict
Plot Events
Resolution

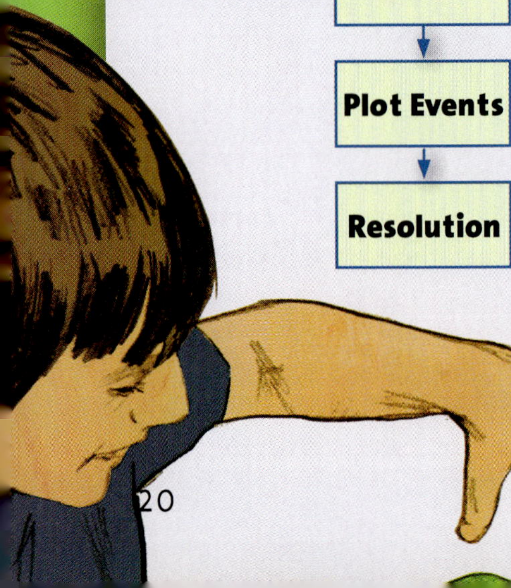

Writing

In Theme 1, you wrote several compositions. In Lesson 5, you will choose one of these compositions to revise. You will choose a composition to revise and publish.

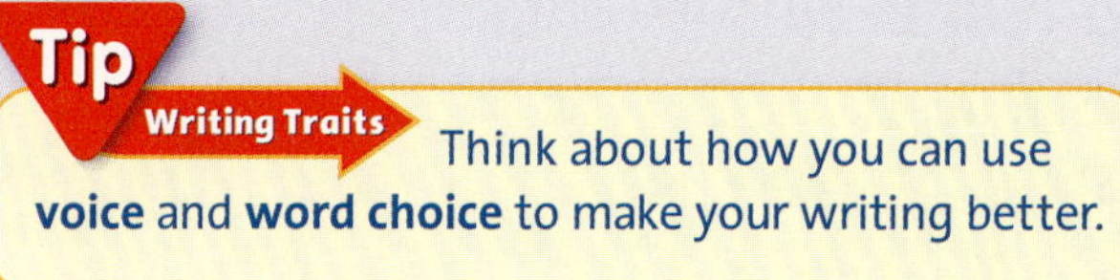

Tip **Writing Traits** Think about how you can use **voice** and **word choice** to make your writing better.

SAMPLE REVISION

Look at how the first paragraph below was revised. What makes the revised paragraph better?

I hear my name being called. It is my turn to go on stage and perform my dance. I am scared. I am afraid I will forget what to do. Everyone will laugh at me.

I hear my name being called. It is the moment I've been afraid of – my turn to go on stage. Suddenly, I can't move. I am frozen with fear. I am sure that when I go on stage, I will forget how to do my dance. My feet will move in the wrong directions, and everyone will laugh at me!

Lesson 6

Background and Vocabulary

Selections You Will Read

- "The Night of San Juan"
- "Tejano Festival

"The Night of San Juan" is realistic fiction. **Realistic fiction**

- has characters and events like those in real life
- includes a setting that could be a real place
- describes challenges and problems that might happen in real life

What is "The Night of San Juan" about?

José Manuel stays on the balcony because his grandmother won't let him play with the rest of the children. Evelyn and her sisters hatch a plan to change his grandmother's mind.

Making a plan means thinking of a way to do something.

Overcoming fear means learning to not feel afraid of someone or something.

Jamie's mother and a flight attendant help her overcome her fear of flying.

What vocabulary will you learn?

Robust Vocabulary

- wistful
- grateful
- grim
- raspy
- swarmed
- revelers
- irresistible

Tip

Be a Word Detective! Look for these words in newspapers, magazines, and books. Listen for the words on the radio or television.

Word Bank

fountain

balcony

wave

ocean

beach

Comprehension

What is the focus skill in this lesson?

The focus skill is **Theme**.

The **theme** is the story message.

A story with a stated theme explains the theme.

You must figure out the theme of a story with an unstated theme. Think about the main characters' thoughts and actions. Also, think about what the main characters learn.

Read the passage.

Maria got her paper back from the new teacher. She had some questions about the teacher's marks, but she was afraid to ask about them. She worried for days. Finally, she gathered the courage to talk to the new teacher. He told her that he liked her writing, and he gave her ideas to make it even better.

The **theme** of the story is that you can learn more by facing fear than running from things that scare you.

Grammar and Writing

What kind of writing will you do in this lesson?

You will write a **personal response paragraph** about a story you have read. You will focus ideas by first telling story events. Then you will tell your thoughts about the story. Here is a short personal response paragraph:

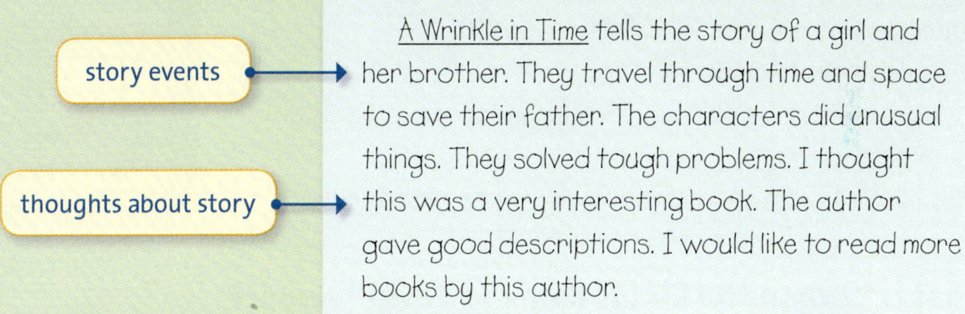

What is the grammar skill?

You will learn about **compound subjects** and **predicates**.

Decoding–Spelling Connection

These words have the /ul/ sound. They are spelled with the final *C –le* pattern.

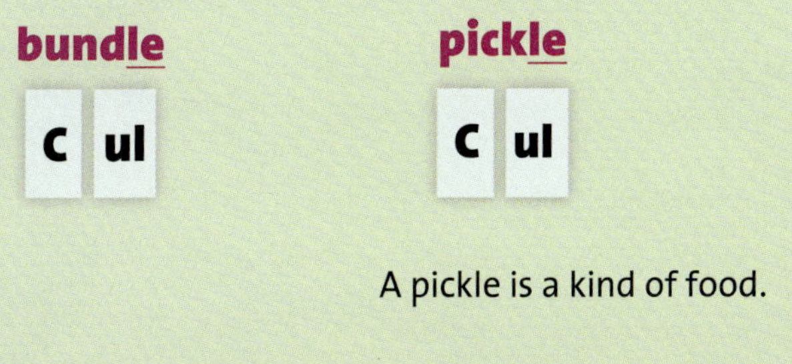

A pickle is a kind of food.

Lesson 7

Background and Vocabulary

Selections You Will Read

- "When the Circus Came to Town"
- "Poetry Beat"

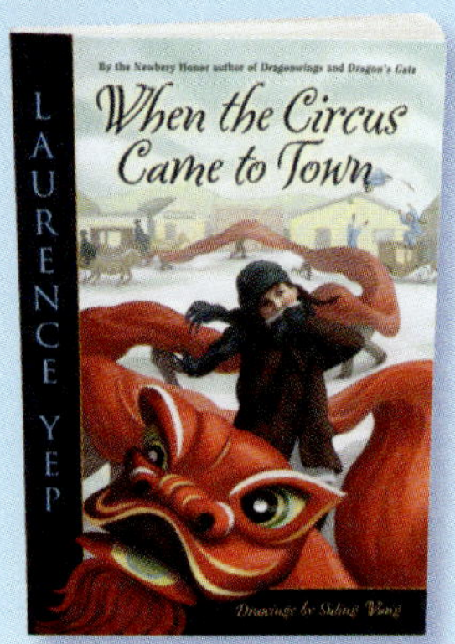

"When the Circus Came to Town" is **historical fiction**. **Historical fiction**

- includes characters who have feelings that real people have
- tells about a main character who overcomes a challenge

What is "When the Circus Came to Town" about?

This selection is about life in the American West. It is also about a child who is embarrassed about her appearance.

Embarrassment about appearance is when a person feels shy or uncomfortable about the way he or she looks.

What vocabulary will you learn?

Robust Vocabulary

- fret
- assured
- nudged
- outlandish
- ruckus
- proclaimed

Tip

As you learn new words, remember to write them in your Vocabulary Log. Which words do you know very well? Which words are you still learning?

Word Bank

circus

clown

unicycle

acrobat

Comprehension

What is the focus skill in this lesson?

The focus skill is **Theme**.

A story's **theme** is its message, or moral.

The **theme** may be stated directly or unstated.

Think about what the main character learns. This will help you figure out an **unstated theme**.

The main character's thoughts and actions help to show the theme. The way the main character solves the problem also helps to show the **theme**.

Read the passage.

Kamal really wanted a ring for his birthday. Kamal was surprised when he found a ring in the park. Then he saw a sign with a drawing of the ring and the phone number of the owner. Kamal wanted the ring for himself. Then he thought about how much it meant to the person who had lost it. He called the owner.

The **theme** of the story is that the right decision might be the choice you would rather not make.

Grammar and Writing

What kind of writing will you do in this lesson?

You will write a **journal entry**. You will focus your ideas in a description. The description will tell your thoughts and feelings during a personal experience. Here is a short journal entry about a personal experience:

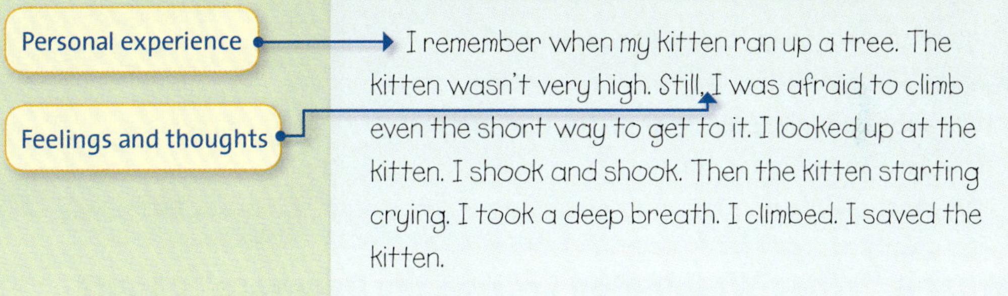

I remember when my kitten ran up a tree. The kitten wasn't very high. Still, I was afraid to climb even the short way to get to it. I looked up at the kitten. I shook and shook. Then the kitten starting crying. I took a deep breath. I climbed. I saved the kitten.

What is the grammar skill?

You will learn about **simple** and **compound sentences**.

The clown smiles. ← simple sentence

compound sentence

The acrobats performed and the crowd cheered.

Decoding–Spelling Connection

These words are spelled with the VCCV pattern. Many words with this pattern are divided into syllables between the consonant pair.

common

VC CV

squirrel

VC CV

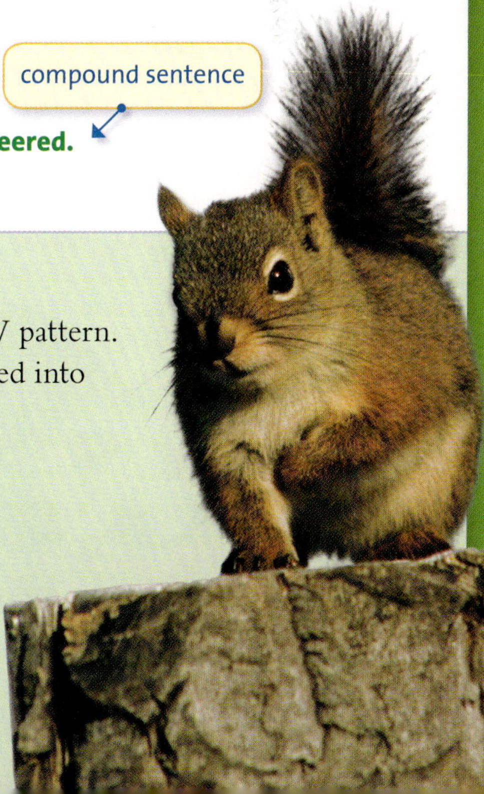

A squirrel is a furry animal.

Lesson 8

Background and Vocabulary

Selections You Will Read

- "When Washington Crossed the Delaware"
- "In 1776"

"When Washington Crossed the Delaware" is **narrative nonfiction**. **Narrative nonfiction**

- tells about people, events, or places that are real
- includes events told in time order
- gives factual information that tells a story

What is "When Washington Crossed the Delaware" about?

This selection is about General George Washington's leadership during the crossing of the Delaware and the battles of Trenton and Princeton.

Strong **leadership** means guiding and organizing followers. A leader helps others to do their best.

The coach leads the team. ▶

What vocabulary will you learn?

Robust Vocabulary

- crucial
- crisis
- maneuvered
- perseverance
- encountered
- persuading
- appealed
- destiny

Tip

Remember to look in the Glossary for explanations of the words. What other strategies can you use?

Word Bank

flags

campfire

bridge

shovel

cannon

Comprehension

What is the focus skill in this lesson?

The focus skill is **Text Structure: Sequence**.

Nonfiction texts often arrange information in **sequence**, or time order.

An author may give dates to show time order. The author may also use time words, such as *first*, *next*, *then*, *finally*, and *the following year.*

When a selection tells events in time order, we say that it has a **text structure** of sequence.

Read the passage.

George Washington never lived in the White House! The White House started being built in 1792. John Adams became U.S. President in 1797. He moved into the White House when it was finished in 1800. The following year, Adams moved out of the White House. 1801 was the same year Thomas Jefferson became president.

This passage is told in time order, or **sequence**. You can see the sequence by looking at the dates.

Grammar and Writing

What kind of writing will you do in this lesson?

You will write a **biography**. You will write important facts about a person's life in time order. Your paragraph will have a main idea, which you will develop with supporting details. Here is a short biography:

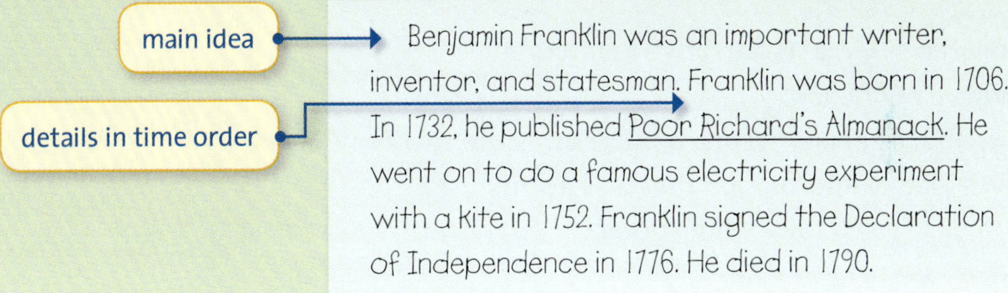

What is the grammar skill?

You will learn about **prepositional phrases**.

Decoding–Spelling Connection

These words are spelled with the VCCV pattern. Many words with this pattern are divided into syllables between the two consonants.

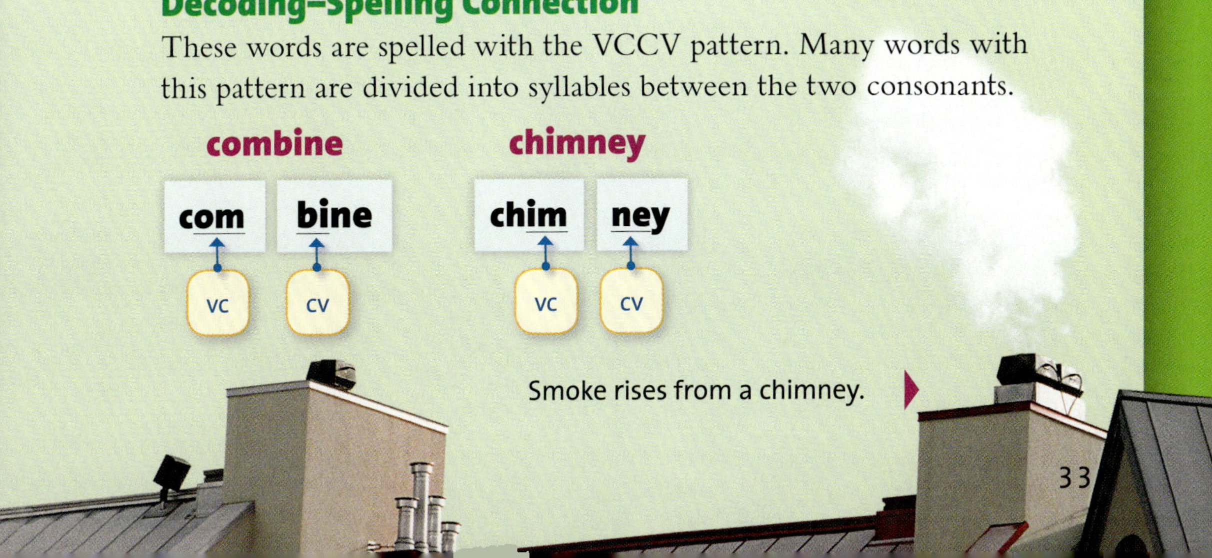

Smoke rises from a chimney.

Lesson 9

Background and Vocabulary

Selections You Will Read

- "Leonardo's Horse"
- "Bellerophon and Pegasus: A Greek Myth"

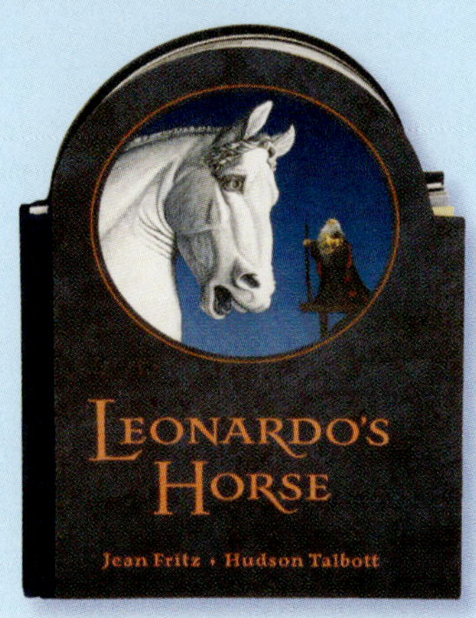

"Leonardo's Horse" is **narrative nonfiction**.
Narrative nonfiction

- tells about people, events, or places that are real
- gives factual information that tells a story
- includes events told in time order

What is "Leonardo's Horse" about?

This selection is about Charles Dent's dream of completing Leonardo da Vinci's unfinished sculpture.

Determination means having a strong purpose and working hard toward a goal.

It takes determination to learn to play the piano well.

What vocabulary will you learn?

Robust Vocabulary

- gesture
- proportion
- resisted
- specialized
- envisioned
- scholars

Tip

As you learn new words, remember to write them in your Vocabulary Log. Which words do you know very well? Which words are you still learning?

Word Bank

Comprehension

What is the focus skill in this lesson?

The focus skill is **Text Structure: Sequence.**

Nonfiction texts often arrange information in **sequence**, or time order.

An author may give dates to show time order. The author may also use time words, such as *first*, *next*, *then*, *finally*, and *the following year.*

When a selection tells events in time order, we say that it has a text structure of sequence.

Read the passage

> I made a dog sculpture in art class. First, I found pictures of dogs. Next, I put clay on my table. Then I shaped my clay like a dog. Finally, I let the clay dry.

This passage is told in time order, or **sequence**. The sequence is indicated by words like *first, next, then,* and *finally.*

Grammar and Writing

What kind of writing will you do in this lesson?

You will write a **summary** of something you have read. You will write the main idea first. Then you will develop it with important details written in time order. Here is a short summary:

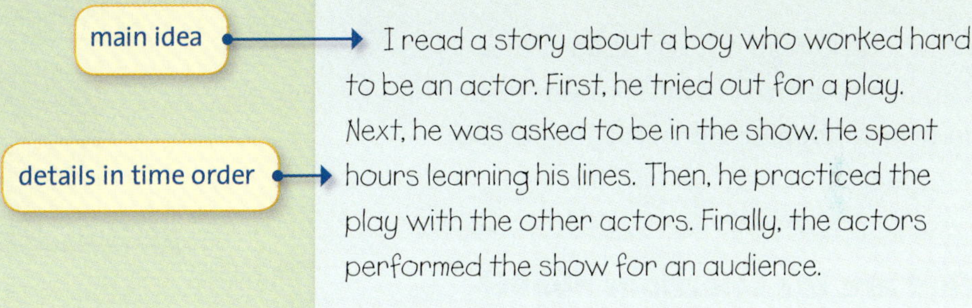

What is the grammar skill?

You will learn about **clauses and phrases** and **complex phrases**.

Decoding–Spelling Connection

Some words are spelled with the VCCCV pattern.

Goggles keep your eyes safe.

Lesson 10

Review

Background and Vocabulary

Selections You Will Read

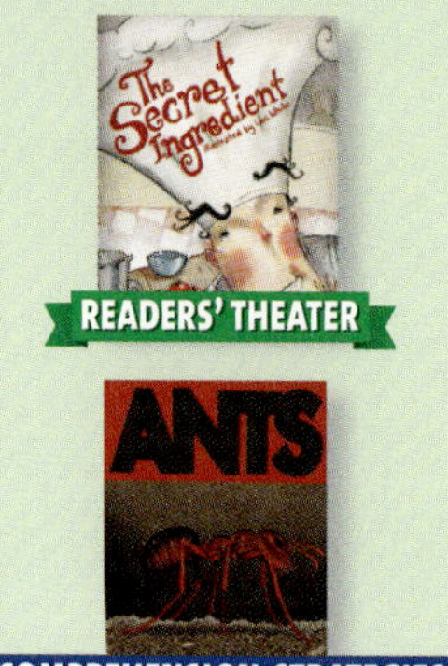

You will read a selection titled "The Secret Ingredient." The selection is a **Readers' Theater**.

READERS' THEATER

You will also read a story titled "Ants." This selection is **expository nonfiction**. Expository nonfiction gives facts and information about a real-life subject.

COMPREHENSION STRATEGIES

What are the selections about?

"**The Secret Ingredient**" is about a cooking show. The cast and crew of the show help their guest find a new special item to put into his chili.

"**Ants**" is about ant colonies and nests. Through labels, keys, and diagrams, the reader gets a close look at ants and the way they live.

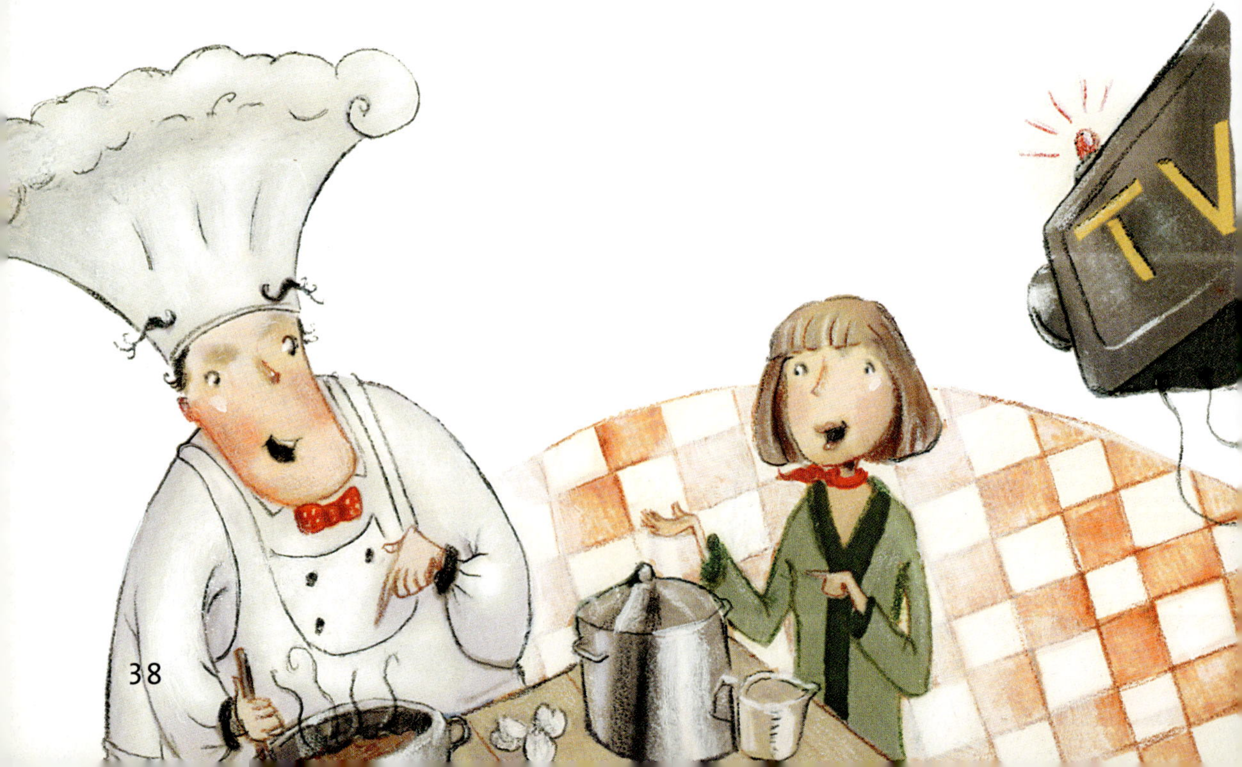

What vocabulary will you learn?

Robust Vocabulary

- eminent
- charity
- modest
- disgruntled
- inadequate
- aghast
- dismayed
- amends
- absentminded
- concoction

Tip

Remember to look in the Glossary for explanations of the words. What other strategies can you use?

Word Bank

chili peppers

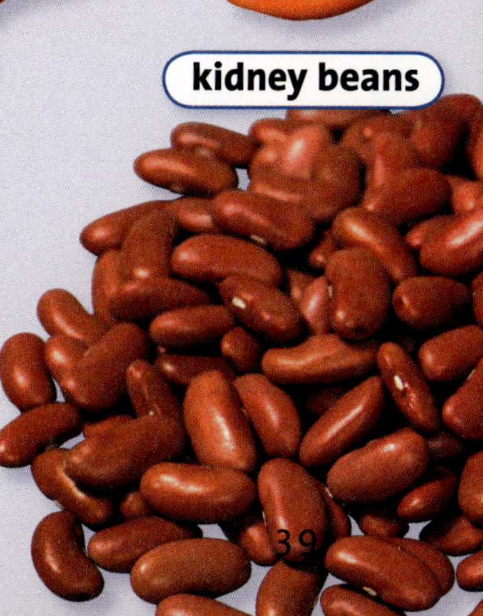

Fluency

As you read "The Secret Ingredient," you will build fluency. When you read a script aloud, remember to

- read with **expression** to add emotion to your lines and to make the characters come alive
- pay attention to **phrasing** by pausing between groups of words that go together

Comprehension Strategies

As you read "Ants," you will review the two comprehension strategies you learned in Theme 2.

- **Ask Questions** Ask yourself questions before, during, and after you read a selection. This will help you understand what you are reading.
- **Use Graphic Organizers** Use graphic organizers to write important ideas. Fill in information about the text as you read.

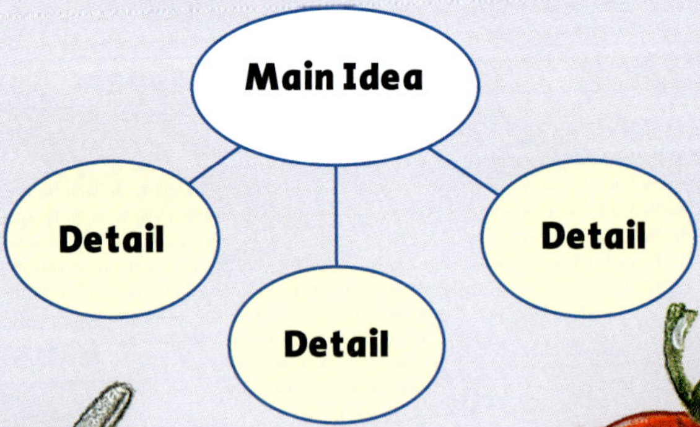

Writing

In Theme 2, you wrote several compositions. In Lesson 10, you will choose one of these compositions to revise. You will choose a composition to revise and publish.

Tip **Writing Traits** Think about how you can use **focus ideas** and use **organization** to make your writing better.

SAMPLE REVISION

Look at how the first paragraph below was revised. What makes the revised paragraph better?

There were ants outside. We were cooking in the kitchen. I closed a window. Our uncle made a delicious soup! Our uncle came over to cook with us. Ants were crawling near the open window.

We had a problem when our uncle came over to cook with us. A window was open, and ants were about to crawl inside onto the counter. I quickly closed the window. Then, our uncle made a delicious soup!

Lesson 11

Background and Vocabulary

Selections You Will Read

- "Sailing Home"
- "Voyage into the Past"

"Sailing Home" is **historical** fiction. **Historical** fiction

- tells about people, events, or places that are real or could be real
- takes place at a real time in the past
- refers to events that may have happened

What is "Sailing Home" about?

This selection is about a girl named Matilda, who helps readers understand what family life is like on a ship that travels around the world.

A **sailing ship** is a large boat that is powered by wind.

What vocabulary will you learn?

Robust Vocabulary

- inflammable
- conducted
- shatter
- broached
- seldom
- dignified
- rowdy

Tip

Be a Word Detective! Look for these words in newspapers, magazines, and books. Listen for the words on the radio or television.

Word Bank

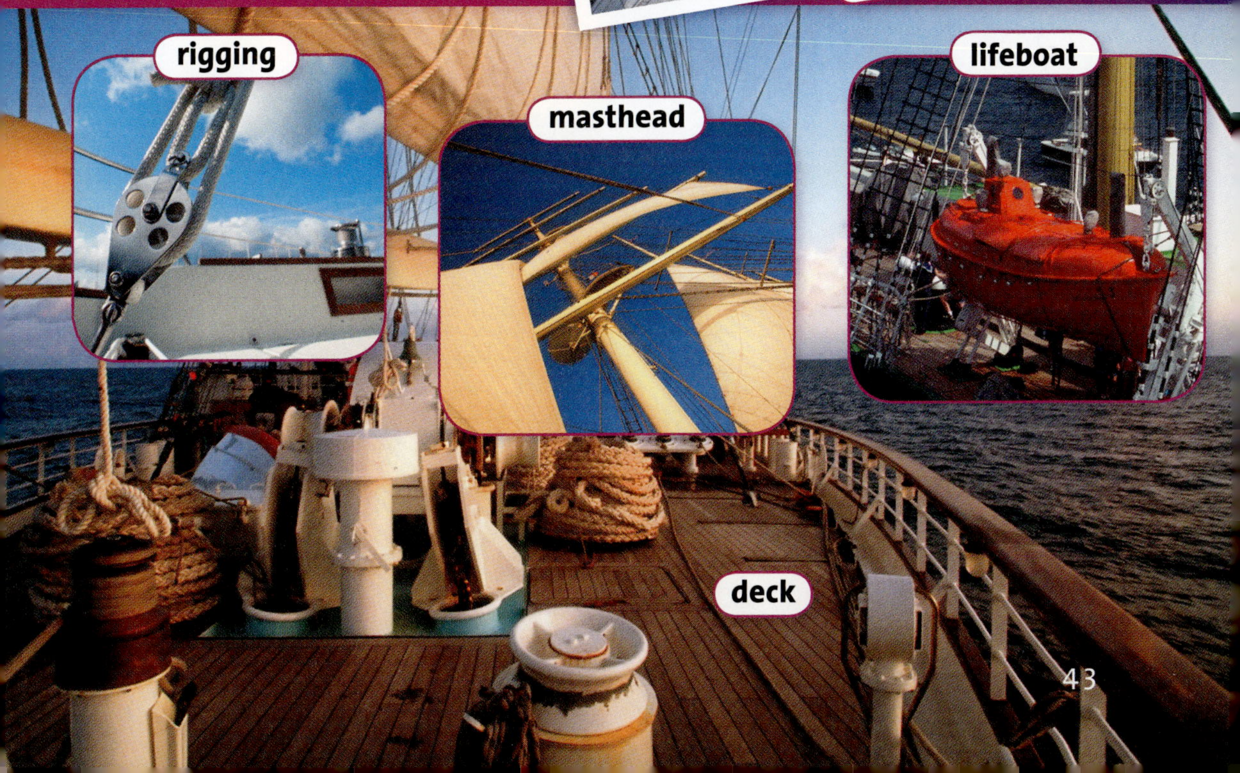

sails

rigging

masthead

lifeboat

deck

Comprehension

What is the focus skill in this lesson?

The focus skill is **Compare and Contrast**.

Historical fiction may compare and contrast characters, events, and settings.

When you **compare**, you show how things are alike.

When you **contrast**, you show how things are different.

Read the passage.

Life onboard the Queen Mary was much like life in a fancy hotel. There were elevators, restaurants, gift shops, a ballroom, and even an indoor swimming pool. You could forget you were in the middle of the ocean, until the "hotel" began to roll from side to side. Then you couldn't even walk without grasping the handrails that lined every corridor. Also, there aren't any hotels that water down the tablecloths to keep the dishes from sliding onto the floor!

The writer **compares** and **contrasts** the Queen Mary to a fancy hotel. First, the writer compares the two by listing the similarities. Then, the writer contrasts the two by listing the differences.

Grammar and Writing

What kind of writing will you do in this lesson?

You will write a **descriptive paragraph**. You should use a variety of sentences types and lengths. Be sure to punctuate correctly. Here is a descriptive paragraph:

The white sails billowed once, and then they caught the breeze. Our tiny boat straightened and began to skim across the smooth, diamond-blue water. I lay back, closed my eyes, and let the warmth of the Caribbean sun sink into my bones. I could hear the thin lines of rigging flapping against the masthead while somewhere, a gull called out. How long would this paradise last? Forever, I hoped.

sights

touch

sounds

What is the grammar skill?

You will learn about **common** and **proper nouns**.

Decoding–Spelling Connection

Syllables that break *before* the next consonant have a long vowel sound, as in *ocean*.

Syllables that break *after* the next consonant have a short vowel sound, as in *minute*.

ocean

o | **cean**

minute

mi | **nute**

An ocean is the largest body of water on Earth.

Lesson 12

Background and Vocabulary

Selections You Will Read

- "Ultimate Field Trip 3"
- "The Florida Everglades"

"Ultimate Field Trip 3" is an **informational narrative**.
An **informational narrative**

- is a story that presents factual information
- involves real people or events
- gives information about a topic

What is "Ultimate Field Trip 3" about?

This selection is about a field trip students take to a tidal zone. Photos and captions show the students studying coastal animal life.

Adaptation is the way an animal adjusts to the changing conditions of its environment.

A **tidal zone** is the area on the shore where the tide moves in and out.

tidal zone

What vocabulary will you learn?

Robust Vocabulary

- adjust
- residents
- specimens
- recoil
- pesky
- internal
- debris

Tip

As you learn new words, remember to write them in your Vocabulary Log. Which words do you know very well? Which words are you still learning?

Word Bank

Comprehension

What is the focus skill in this lesson?

The focus skill is **Text Structure: Compare and Contrast**.

Narratives may have a compare-and-contrast text structure.

When you **compare**, you show how things are alike.

When you **contrast**, you show how things are different.

When a selection uses compare and contrast, we say it has a text structure of compare and contrast.

Read the passsage.

Dulse and kelp are two kinds of algae that grow in seawater. Dulse is a red alga found along the shores of Maine. It is used in foods and medicines. Sundried dulse is ground into powder, flakes, or is fried into chips. Unlike dulse, kelp is a flat, brown alga that grows off Vancouver Island. Kelp contains algin, an ingredient used in ice cream and toothpaste to give them texture. Kelp is also used as fertilizer.

The writer compares and contrasts dulse and kelp. The writer compares the two by talking about how they are both algae that grow in seawater. The writer contrasts the two by talking about the different places they grow and the different uses of kelp and dulse.

Grammar and Writing

What kind of writing will you do in this lesson?

You will write a **compare-and-contrast paragraph**. You must use a combination of simple, compound, and complex sentences that are punctuated correctly. Here is a compare-and-contrast paragraph:

This is a comparison.

This is a contrast.

Within the tidal zone there are actually six different zones. Each zone supports animal life, but the animals differ from zone to zone depending on the depth of water. Animals that can survive underwater longer live closer to the ocean, while animals that can survive underwater only a short time live closer to the shore.

What is the grammar skill?

You will learn about **singular nouns** and **plural nouns**.

plural noun

singular noun

Decoding–Spelling Connection

The prefix *un-* means "not."

unwise

un | **wise**

undesirable

un | **desirable**

It is unwise to drive on a flat tire.

Lesson 13

Background and Vocabulary

Selections You Will Read

- "Stormalong"
- "Paul Bunyan Makes Progress"

"Stormalong" is a **tall tale**. A **tall tale**

- is a humorous story about impossible events
- exaggerates the strengths and abilities of a character
- is often found in stories and legends about American folk heroes

What is "Stormalong" about?

This selection is the tale of Stormy the sailor, who feels he doesn't fit in, no matter where he lives. The story follows his adventures and tells what cures his loneliness.

An **exaggeration** is a description in terms that are larger-than-life.

A **hero** is a person who is famous, courageous, and noble.

What vocabulary will you learn?

Robust Vocabulary

- bellowing
- outcast
- reputation
- betrayed
- yearning
- withered
- escapades
- unfathomable

Tip

Be a Word Detective! Look for these words in newspapers, magazines, and books. Listen for the words on the radio or television.

Word Bank

cargo

anchor

oar

hammock

Comprehension

What is the focus skill in this lesson?

The focus skill is **Cause and Effect**.

Tall tales sometimes use cause and effect to make connections between ideas.

A **cause** makes something happen.
An **effect** is what happens.

A selection may use causes and effects to make connections between ideas.

Read the passage.

A big farm is a lot of work, but a vegetable garden is a lot of fun. My favorite area of the garden is the potato patch. Each year, warm temperatures, spring rain, and bright sunshine bring forth the deep green leaves and stems of the potato plants. By midsummer, you can reach into the soil and uncover a cluster of pale yellow baby potatoes. There is nothing as delicious as Yukon Golds dug fresh from the garden.

The writer has used cause-and-effect to describe how potatoes grow. The cause of their growth is warm temperatures, rain, and sunshine. The effects are the plants and the potatoes.

Grammar and Writing

What kind of writing will you do in this lesson?

You will write a **description of a character**. Your character description must use conventions, which are complete sentences that have correct grammar, spelling, punctuation, and capitalization. Here is a paragraph that describes a character:

details about qualities

details about interests

German Shepherds are known for their intelligence, and Wrigley was definitely smart, but his best qualities were his loving nature and his passion for fun. When he wasn't romping at his favorite places, the beach and the dog park, he'd sneak into our rooms and steal the pillows off our beds. He did anything to make us laugh and give him a hug.

What is the grammar skill?

You will learn about **possessive nouns**.

Stormy's oar is broken.

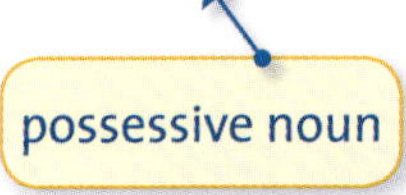

Decoding–Spelling Connection

The suffix *–less* means "without".

ageless

age	less

motionless

mo	tion	less

A car that is parked is motionless.

Lesson 14

Background and Vocabulary

Selections You Will Read

- "A Drop of Water"
- "Rain, Dance! Steam. Ice Cycle"

"A Drop of Water" is **expository nonfiction**.

Expository nonfiction

- gives facts and information about a topic
- has headings that begin sections of related information
- has a text structure—the way the ideas and information are organized

What is "A Drop of Water" about?

This selection is about the nature of water. It explains how ice, vapor, frost, and dew are all formed by water molecules.

Forms of Water are liquid, solid, and gas. Water can be explained by its smallest part, molecules.

▲ Liquid

▲ Solid

▲ Gas

What vocabulary will you learn?

Robust Vocabulary

- elongates
- elastic
- rigid
- accumulate
- underlying
- intricate
- vanish
- replenishing

Tip

Remember to look in the glossary for explanations of the words. What other strategies can you use?

Word Bank

sphere

water molecule

snowflake

dew

frost

Comprehension

What is the focus skill in this lesson?

The focus skill is **Text Structure: Cause and Effect**.

Nonfiction sometimes tells about causes and effects.

A **cause** makes something happen.

An **effect** is what happens.

When a selection uses many causes and effects, we say that it has a **text structure** of cause and effect.

Read the passage.

A flash flood happens when a slow-moving thunderstorm passes over an area with many streambeds. Because the thunderstorm is slow-moving, the area receives extra heavy amounts of rain. The small streams become overfilled with rainwater. They grow into wide and deep speeding rivers that destroy vegetation and buildings along the embankment. The floods are called flash floods because they develop so quickly.

The writer uses cause-and-effect to explain what happens in a flash flood. The cause of a flash flood is a slow-moving thunderstorm. The effect is swollen streams and damage.

Grammar and Writing

What kind of writing will you do in this lesson?

You will write a **cause-and-effect paragraph**. Your paragraph must use correct grammar, spelling, punctuation, and capitalization. You will organize your writing with causes and effects. Here is a cause-and-effect paragraph:

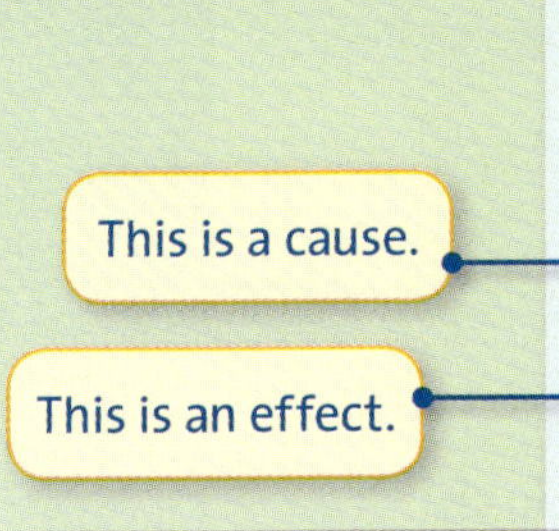

Water can take many forms. It can be water, ice, or vapor. The temperature of the air causes water molecules to gain or lose energy. When the temperature is warm, water molecules gain energy and form vapor. When the temperature is cold, water molecules lose energy and form ice.

What is the grammar skill?

You will learn about **pronouns** and **antecedents**.

Snowflakes take different shapes as they float down to earth.

Decoding–Spelling Connection

The /ən/ sound can be spelled *on* or *en*.

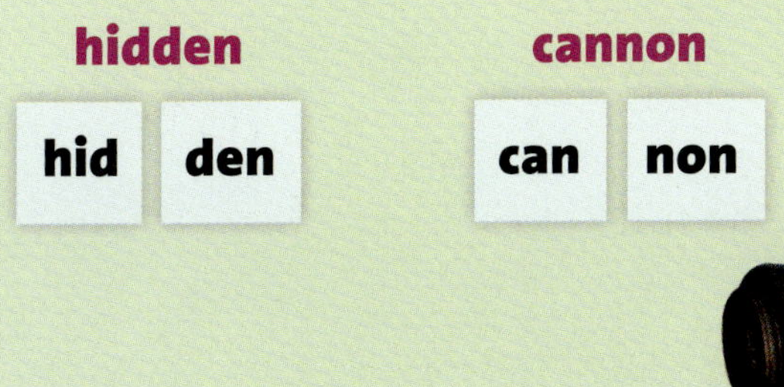

A cannon is a large gun on wheels.

Lesson 15

Review

Background and Vocabulary

Selections You Will Read

You will read a selection titled "How the Prairie Became Ocean." The selection is a **Readers' Theater**.

You will also read a selection titled "How Does Ocean Water Move?" This selection is from a **textbook**. Textbooks give facts and information about a topic.

COMPREHENSION STRATEGIES

What are the selections about?

"**How the Prairie Became Ocean**" is about Yurok children who are kept awake by a nighttime storm. They listen as their grandmother tells a creation myth.

"**How Does Ocean Water Move?**" is about waves and currents. Text features such as headings, charts, and diagrams help students understand that ocean water is in constant motion.

ocean waves

What vocabulary will you learn?

Robust Vocabulary

recount	parched
uninhabitable	sorrowful
sustain	
monotonous	
endeavor	
dwell	
brimming	
teeming	

Tip

Remember to look in the Glossary for explanations of the words. What other strategies can you use?

Word Bank

sea lion

abalone shell

salmon

lodge

whale

Fluency

As you read "How the Prairie Became Ocean" you will build fluency. When reading a script aloud, remember to

- change your **intonation** to show the different feelings your character is experiencing
- adjust your **pace** to match the action in the play

Comprehension Strategies

As you read "How Does Ocean Water Move," you will review the two comprehension strategies you learned in Theme 3.

- **Monitor Comprehension: Self-Correct** It is important to monitor your own comprehension as you read. Use self-correction strategies such as decoding longer words to improve your understanding.
- **Use Graphic Organizers** Use graphic organizers to show how authors organize important ideas into text structures, such as cause and effect, compare and contrast, or sequence.

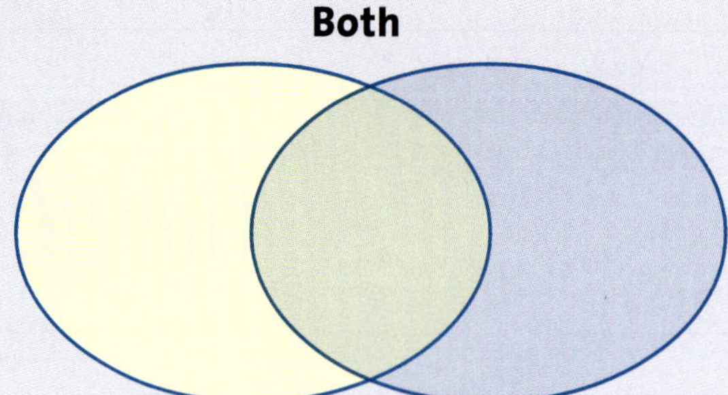

Writing

In Theme 3, you wrote several compositions. In Lesson 15, you will choose one of these compositions to revise. You will choose a composition to revise and publish.

Tip **Writing Traits** Think about how you can use **different sentence types** and **writing conventions** to make your writing better.

SAMPLE REVISION

Look at how the first paragraph below was revised. What makes the revised paragraph better?

I like to jump the waves at the beach. i like it because the waves lift me up and down. It's really fun when a big waves comes

What's my favorite thing to do at the ocean? It's to stand in the water up to my chin and jump up just as a big wave rolls over me. I love the feeling of weightlessness as the huge wave lifts me higher and higher.

Lesson 16

Background and Vocabulary

What is the main selection?

- "The School Story"
- "How Anansi Gave the World Stories"

"The School Story" is **realistic fiction**. Realistic fiction

- has characters who have feelings that real people have
- has conflicts that might happen in real life

What is "The School Story" about?

When Natalie gets her first children's story published, she learns a lot about the publishing process.

An **editor** works with a writer to make the book better.

Publishing is the business of producing and selling books. After a book is published, you can buy it in a bookstore.

What vocabulary will you learn?

Robust Vocabulary

- tempted
- insights
- essence
- indication
- proposed
- instinct
- baffled

As you learn new words, remember to write them down in your Vocabulary Log. Which words do you know very well? Which words are you still learning?

Word Bank

invitation

review

handwriting

Dear Grandpa,
I had such a great time on our fishing trip. I can't believe I caught a big fish. I'm coming to see you in two weeks. I can't wait to see you. The party is going to be so much fun.
Love You,
Emilio

catalog

Comprehension

What is the focus skill in this lesson?

The focus skill is **Make Inferences**.

Realistic fiction has characters and events that are like people and events in real life.

When we **make inferences**, we use information from the story and our own experiences to figure out something that the author has not explained.

Read the passage.

After working long and hard on her short story, Katy was ready to submit it to the editor. She took her short story to the publishing office to meet Mrs. Durning, who would edit the story before it was published. As Katy approached her office, she saw that Mrs. Durning was a very serious, older woman who looked intimidating. Katy stopped suddenly and hid behind a filing cabinet."

The author of the passage does not say it, but you can make the inference that Katy is nervous about meeting the editor. You can use your own experience to figure out that Katy felt scared and uneasy about meeting someone much older than herself.

Grammar and Writing

What kind of writing will you do in this lesson?

You will write a **narrative scene** that has conversation between two characters. You learn about people from what they say and how they say it. You learn about characters in a story the same way. Each character in the scene should have a distinct voice.

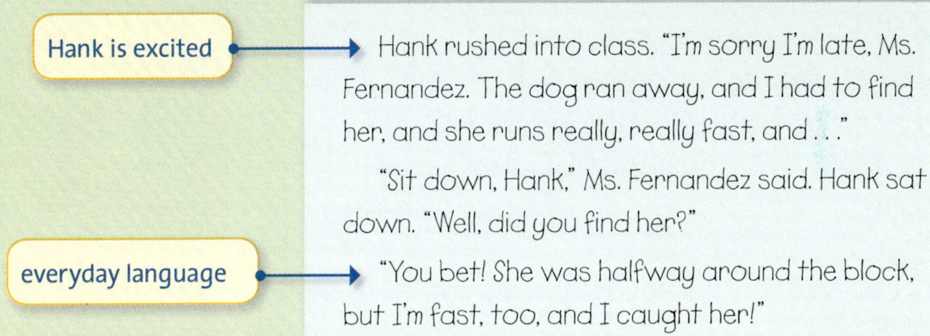

What is the grammar skill?

You will learn about **subject** and **object pronouns**.

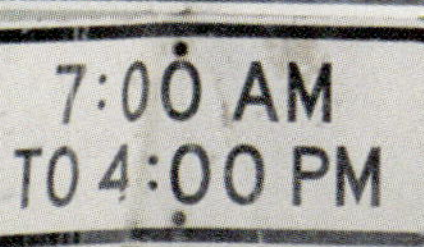

Decoding–Spelling Connection

Prefixes such as *im-*, *in-*, and *il-* can be added to root words. Sometimes when the prefix is added to the root word, there will be two of the same consonant.

It is illegal to drive faster than 15 miles per hour near a school.

Lesson 17

Background and Vocabulary

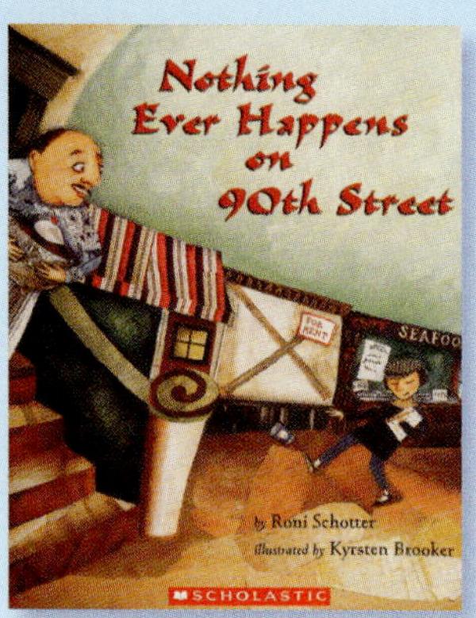

Selections You Will Read

- "Nothing Ever Happens on 90th Street"
- "The Artist's Eye"

"Nothing Ever Happens on 90th Street" is **realistic fiction**. Realistic fiction

- has characters who behave like real people
- has characters with problems that might happen in real life

What is "Nothing Ever Happens on 90th Street" about?

Eva is a young writer who has run out of ideas. Then her neighbors help her find a story to tell.

Observation is the art of watching carefully. When you observe people, you pay close attention to everything they do.

Imagination is what you use when you make something up. Children use their imaginations when they play.

What vocabulary will you learn?

Robust Vocabulary

- hiatus
- embarked
- unimaginable
- extravagant
- gourmet
- throng
- precarious

Tip

Remember to look in the glossary for explanations of the words. What other strategies can you use?

Word Bank

pigeon

chef

embrace

stage

Comprehension

What is the focus skill in this lesson?

The focus skill is **Make Inferences**.

When we **make inferences**, we use story clues and our own experiences to figure out something that the author has not explained.

Read the passage.

Mimi was looking for a photo of her great grandmother to put in a story she was writing about her family. Mimi spent hours looking through family photos but could not find a single photo of her great grandmother. She was frustrated and could not think of anything to put in place of the photo. Mimi was just about to give up altogether when her mother gave her an old locket that contained a photo of Mimi's great grandmother. Mimi squeezed her mother's hand.

Even though the author does not say it, we can make the inference that Mimi was very happy to receive her mother's locket. You can use your own experience with finding what you are looking for to understand how happy Mimi was.

Grammar and Writing

What kind of writing will you do in this lesson?

You will write a **skit**. A skit is a short, funny play that involves a conversation between characters. The conversation should sound natural, as if real people were talking. The words you choose for the characters to say reflect your voice as the writer. They also reveal what the characters are like. Here is a short skit:

Natural, everyday language

"Danny, get up! You're sitting on my hat," Carol said.

"Your hat! I thought it was a cushion. I'm sorry," Danny said.

"You should be sorry. It's my favorite hat," Carol said.

"Maybe now it will be your favorite cushion," Danny said.

What is the grammar skill?

You will learn about **possessive and reflexive pronouns**.

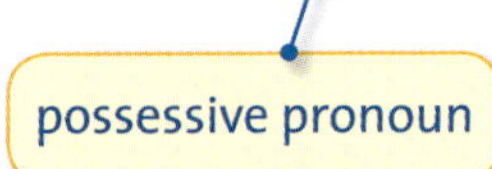

Decoding–Spelling Connection

Suffixes such as *-ant* and *-ist* can be added to root words.

accountant		artist	
account	ant	art	ist

The artist is painting a portrait.

Lesson 18

Background and Vocabulary

Selections You Will Read

- "Project Mulberry"
- "Journey on the Silk Road"

"Project Mulberry" is **realistic fiction**. Realistic fiction

- has characters who have feelings that real people have
- has characters with problems that might happen in real life

What is "Project Mulberry" about?

Even though Patrick is afraid of worms, he and his friend Julia decide to raise caterpillars for "Project Mulberry". As they watch the caterpillars go through their life cycles, they face problems and find solutions.

Life cycle means the different stages an animal or plant goes through over its life. During a butterfly's life cycle, it goes through four stages.

The chrysalis is the second stage.

The final stage of the butterfly's life cycle.

What vocabulary will you learn?

Robust Vocabulary

- compartments
- swayed
- phobia
- invasion
- vetoed
- wispy

Tip

Be a Word Detective! Look for these words in newspapers, magazines, and books. Listen for the words on the radio or television.

Word Bank

aquarium

hammock

cocoon

caterpillar

Comprehension

What is the focus skill in this lesson?

The focus skill is **Main Ideas and Details.**

Realistic fiction sometimes gives facts about a topic. These facts are often organized into a **main idea** and supporting **details**.

The **main idea** is the most important idea in a paragraph or section. **Details** are information that supports the **main idea**.

Read the passage.

For my science fair project, I studied hydroponics. Hydroponics is the method of growing plants without soil. Instead of getting nutrients from soil, plants get them from water that has nutrients in it. The idea is that the plants can get nutrients more easily, so they do less work and grow faster. Hydroponics can be used in places where traditional methods of growing plants are not possible, like the South Pole and maybe even in space someday.

The main idea of this passage is that hydroponics allows you to grow plants in water. Details about how hydroponics works and why hydroponics is an important method of growing plants support the main idea.

Grammar and Writing

What kind of writing will you do in this lesson?

You will write a **suspense story**. Writers create suspense by choosing their words carefully. A suspense story needs words that express action and create a sense of tension. This is the beginning of a suspense story.

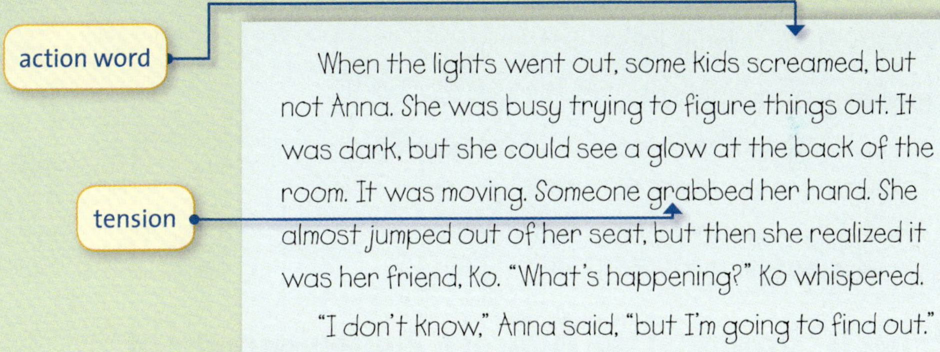

What is the grammar skill?

You will learn about **adjectives** and **articles**.

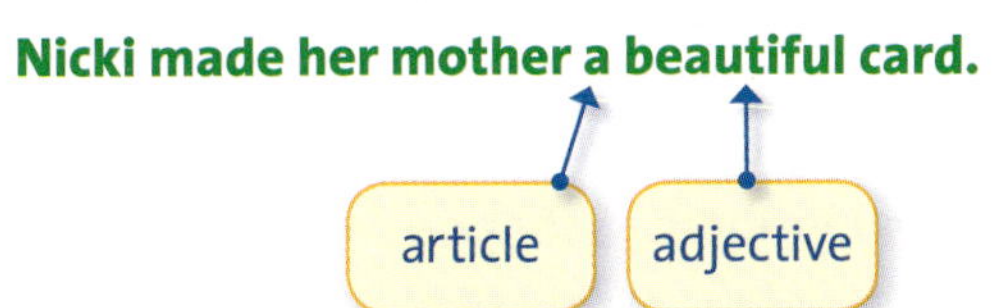

Decoding–Spelling Connection

Suffixes such as *-ous* and *-ious* can be added to root words. Sometimes the spelling of the root word changes when the suffix is added.

mountainous

mountain | **ous**

gracious

grace | **ious**

Lesson 19

Background and Vocabulary

Selections You Will Read

- "Inventing the Future: A Photobiography of Thomas Alva Edison"
- "Letter from Thomas Edison to Henry Ford"

"Inventing the Future: A Photobiography of Thomas Alva Edison" is a **biography**. A **biography**

- is the story of a person's life, told by someone else
- has details about why the person is important
- shows events in the person's life in time order

What is "Inventing the Future: A Photobiography of Thomas Alva Edison" about?

This selection is about the life of Thomas Alva Edison. It tells about his boyhood, his first jobs, and his early inventions.

Invention means a new device or process created by study and experimentation. An invention can change the way people live.

Thomas Edison invented the first practical light bulb.

What vocabulary will you learn?

Robust Vocabulary

- tendency
- device
- feat
- industry
- irrepressible
- prestigious

Tip

As you learn new words, remember to write them in your Vocabulary Log. Which words do you know very well? Which words are you still learning?

Word Bank

printing press

patent

laboratory

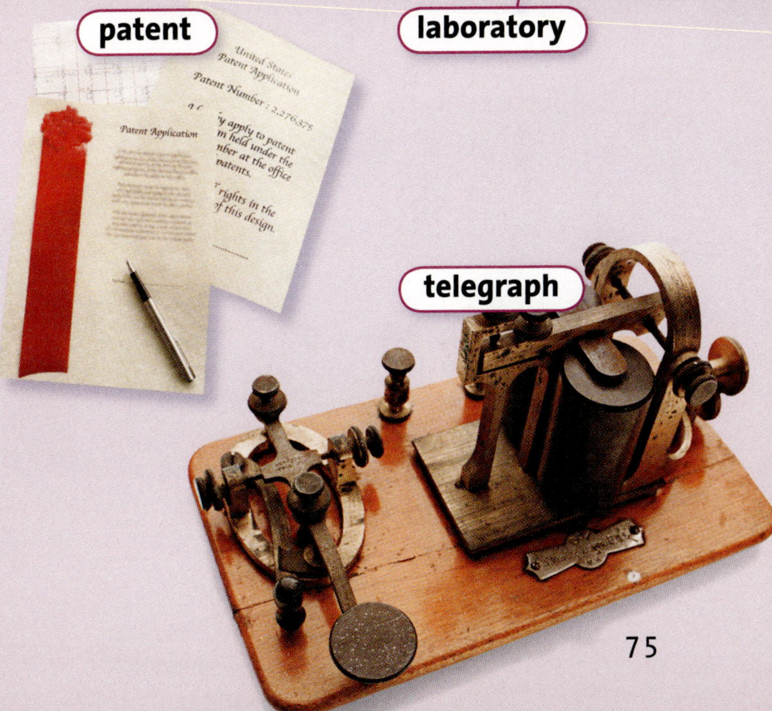

telegraph

Comprehension

What is the focus skill in this lesson?

The focus skill is **Main Ideas and Details**.

A **biography** gives facts about the life and work of an important person. These facts are often organized into a main idea and supporting details.

The **main idea** is the most important idea in a paragraph or section.

The supporting **details** tell more about the **main idea**.

Read the passage.

Although many people know Benjamin Franklin as one of the founding fathers of the United States, he was much more than that. He is credited with being the first person to use a cartoon to express a political idea. He organized the first postal service and was an author and a publisher. He invented bifocal glasses, the odometer, swim flippers, and the lightning rod.

The main idea is that Benjamin Franklin was more than just a founding father of the United States. This is supported by details about his life, such as the different things he invented.

Grammar and Writing

What kind of writing will you do in this lesson?

You will write a **letter to request something**. If you are asking for something, you should use polite, formal language. Your language should be specific, so the person reading it knows exactly what you want and why. Here is a letter requesting something.

Dear Principal Ozawa:

We are the students in Mr. Hickam's fifth grade class. We are writing to ask if we can sell cotton candy at the school fair this year. We will give the money to a local charity that finds homes for abandoned animals. We will work hard to make the cotton candy booth a success. Thank you for considering our request.

Mr. Hickam's fifth grade class

clear intent

polite language

What is the grammar skill?

You will learn about **main verbs** and **helping verbs**.

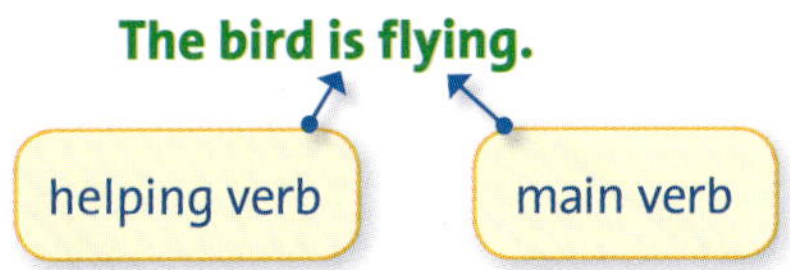

Decoding–Spelling Connection

Words that sound the same but have different spellings and meanings are called *homophones*.

flower		flour
flow	er	flour

The rose is my favorite flower.

Lesson 20

Review

Background and Vocabulary

Selections You Will Read

You will read a selection titled "The Invention Convention." The selection is a **Readers' Theater**.

You will also read a selection titled "When Our Family Bands Together." This selection is **poetry**. Poetry is writing told in verse that is rich in imagery and figurative language.

What are the selections about?

"**The Invention Convention**" is about a convention event that lets audience members vote for the "Invention of the Year."

"**When Our Family Bands Together**" is about a musical celebration when siblings trade places with their parents and play instruments.

musical intruments

What vocabulary will you learn?

Robust Vocabulary

- scours
- appropriate
- practical
- portable
- circulate
- protrude
- boisterous
- deduction
- fickle
- measly

Tip

Be a Word Detective! Look for these words in newspapers, magazines, and books. Listen for the words on the radio or television.

Word Bank

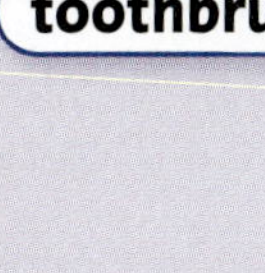

toothbrush

audience

judge

alarm clock

collar

Fluency

As you read "The Invention Convention" you will build fluency. When you read a script aloud, remember to

- choose a **reading rate** that helps your listeners understand the lines you read
- change your **intonation** to show the different feelings your character has

Comprehension Strategies

As you read "When Our Family Bands Together" you will review the two comprehension strategies you learned in Theme 4.

- **Use Story Structure** Identify the characters, setting, and events helps you understand what you are reading.
- **Monitor Comprehension: Adjust Reading Rate** Monitor your comprehension as you read by adjusting your reading rate. Slow down or speed up to match the difficulty of the text.

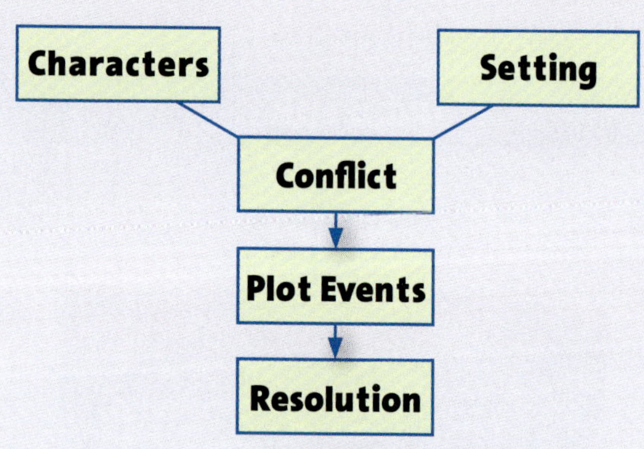

Writing

In Theme 4, you wrote several compositions. In Lesson 20, you will choose one of these compositions to revise. You will choose a composition to revise and publish.

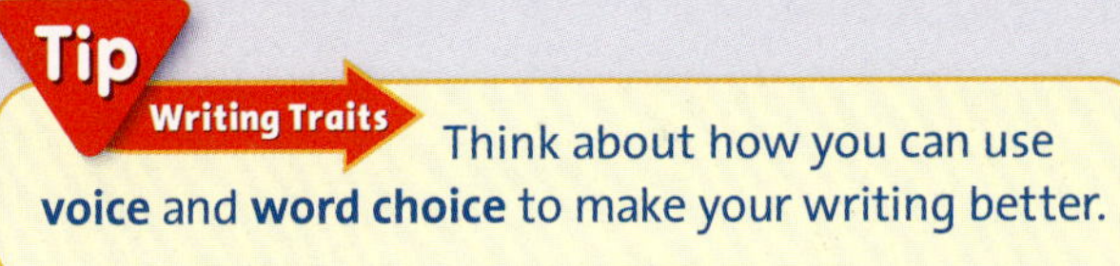

SAMPLE REVISION

Look at how the first paragraph below was revised. What makes the revised paragraph better?

The saxophone was invented by a man named Adolph Sax. Sax played a few instruments. He wanted an instrument that would be like a wind instrument but would have the power of a brass instrument.

Adolph Sax invented my favorite instrument, the saxophone. Sax played the flute and the clarinet, which are wind instruments. He wanted a new instrument, one with the delicacy of a woodwind and the power of a brass instrument. The saxophone combined the best of both!

Lesson 21

Background and Vocabulary

Selections You Will Read

- "Interrupted Journey"
- "Kids in Action"

"Interrupted Journey" is **expository nonfiction**.

Expository nonfiction

- gives facts and information about a topic
- has headings that begin sections of related information

What is "Interrupted Journey" about?

This selection is about the rescue, recovery, and release of an endangered sea turtle.

Rescue means the act of saving something or someone from a harmful situation.

Recovery means the return to normal health of something or someone who was ill or injured.

What vocabulary will you learn?

Robust Vocabulary

- basking
- sleek
- vital
- analyzing
- detect
- damage

Tip

Remember to look in the Glossary for explanations of the words. What other strategies can you use?

Word Bank

Comprehension

What is the focus skill in this lesson?

The focus skill is **Author's Purpose and Perspective**. **Nonfiction** is often written to inform or to persuade.

An **author's purpose** is the reason she or he writes a selection. An author may have more than one purpose.

An **author's perspective** is the opinion she or he has about the topic.

Readers can use clues and details in the text to determine the **author's purpose and perspective**.

Read the passage.

When I was a child, my older brother rescued a bird that had a broken wing. He helped its wing to heal and fed it until it was able to fly again and get its own food. Now when I see a hurt animal, I see if it has an injury that I can heal. If I can, I take it in to my home and help it get better, just like my older brother did. I think everyone should help hurt animals.

One of the author's purposes in writing this passage is to show the reader what her brother taught her about helping animals. The author states her opinion, or perspective, that everyone should help hurt animals.

Grammar and Writing

What kind of writing will you do in this lesson?

You will write a **persuasive letter**. You will use a variety of sentence types to make the letter interesting and persuasive.

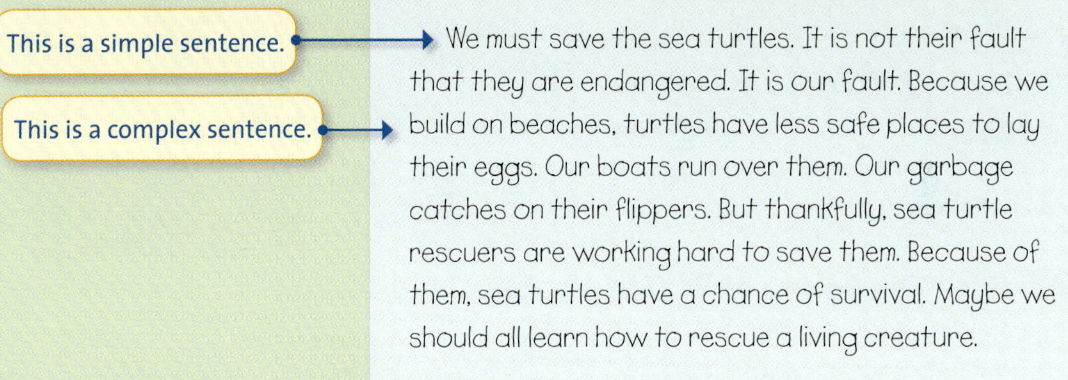

We must save the sea turtles. It is not their fault that they are endangered. It is our fault. Because we build on beaches, turtles have less safe places to lay their eggs. Our boats run over them. Our garbage catches on their flippers. But thankfully, sea turtle rescuers are working hard to save them. Because of them, sea turtles have a chance of survival. Maybe we should all learn how to rescue a living creature.

What is the grammar skill?

You will learn about **action and linking verbs**.

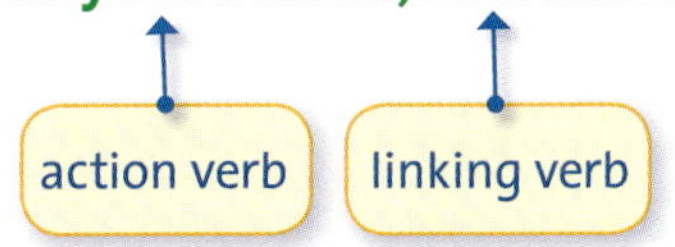

Decoding–Spelling Connection

When the prefixes *in-*, *out-*, *down-*, and *up-* are added to a root word, the spelling of that word does not change.

invertebrate

in **vertebrate**

outgoing

A snail is an invertebrate. ▲

Lesson 22

Background and Vocabulary

Selections You Will Read

- "The Power of W.O.W.!"
- "Got a Problem? Get a Plan!"

"The Power of W.O.W.!" is a **play**. A play

- is a story that can be performed for an audience
- has plot events organized into acts and scenes
- uses dialogue to show characters' actions and feelings

What is "The Power of W.O.W.!" about?

This selection tells about several children who work to save a neighborhood bookmobile program.

Neighborhood means a local community with its own special qualities.

What vocabulary will you learn?

Robust Vocabulary

- somberly
- stammers
- monopolize
- deflated
- enraptured
- enterprising
- cumbersome

Tip

Remember to look in the Glossary for explanations of the words. What other strategies can you use?

Word Bank

reporter

library

car wash

advertisement

Comprehension

What is the focus skill in this lesson?

The focus skill is **Author's Purpose and Perspective**. An author's purpose is the reason she or he writes a selection. An author may want to entertain, inform, and convince — all in the same selection. An author's perspective is her or his opinion on the subject.

Readers can look for clues and details in the text to find the **author's purpose and perspective**.

Read the passage.

Did you ever wonder what it means to help the community? It may sound kind of vague, but there are many things you can do. You could volunteer at a home for the elderly, where you can help with activities or snacks. You can help out at an animal shelter, petting the cats and dogs, cleaning cages, or feeding the animals. You can get involved in cleaning up a local park.

This passage shows the author's purpose, which is to provide information about ways to help out in your community.

Grammar and Writing

What kind of writing will you do in this lesson?

You will write a **persuasive paragraph**. You will write sentences with opinions, reasons, details, and examples to convince the reader.

What is the grammar skill?

You will learn about **present tense and subject-verb agreement**.

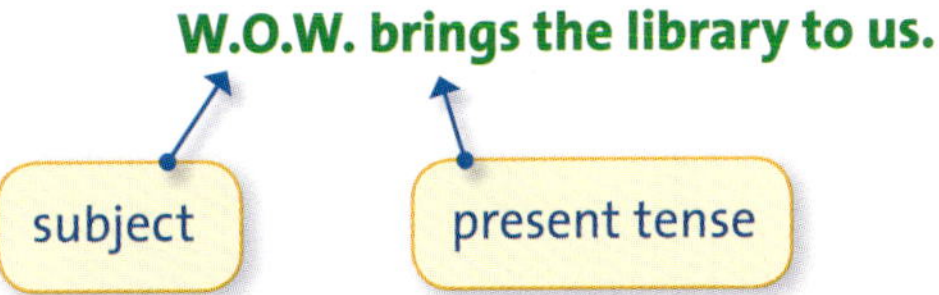

Decoding–Spelling Connection

When the suffixes *–ation*, *–ition*, *–sion* and *–ion* are added to a root word, the spelling of the root word changes.

tension		demolition	
tense	**-sion**	**demolish**	**-ion**

The city ordered the demolition of this building.

Lesson 23

Background and Vocabulary

Selections You Will Read

- "Any Small Goodness"
- "Aesop's Fables"

"Any Small Goodness" is **realistic fiction**. Realistic fiction

- has characters and events like people and events in real life
- has challenges and problems that might happen in real life
- has characters with realistic traits

What is "Any Small Goodness" about?

This selection tells about how a family's search for their lost cat leads them to discover a man of good character.

Character means qualities that make somebody interesting and special.

Doing kind things shows that Jesse has good character.

What vocabulary will you learn?

Robust Vocabulary

- gouges
- desolate
- bustles
- fervor
- immaculate
- assuage

Tip

Remember to look in the Glossary for explanations of the words. What other strategies can you use?

Word Bank

avocado

trout

tweed

bark

lime

Comprehension

What is the focus skill in this lesson?

The focus skill is **Literary Devices**.

Literary devices include **imagery** that makes writing interesting and colorful.

Imagery uses vivid language to describe people, places, things, and ideas. Sensory language is imagery that appeals to the five senses: sight, hearing, smell, taste, and touch.

Readers can look in the text for **literary devices** like imagery.

Read the passage.

We were four generations, sitting around the table in the soft candlelight. Nana, our grandmother, was there with her cloud of silver hair, her red lipstick, her white sweater and old silver pin. My father, her son, sat next to her with his flourish of wavy black hair, and his face a thinner, darker version of hers. My sister was smiling, her soft cheeks and arched eyebrows just like Nana's, only fifty years younger. Finally, there was my niece whose apple cheeks and dark eyes fit right into the family.

This passage uses **imagery** to help the reader imagine the scene and the people in it. Imagery like the soft candlelight appeals to the reader's sense of sight.

Grammar and Writing

What kind of writing will you do in this lesson?

You will write **poetry with persuasive elements**. You will use development to persuade by presenting your topic at the beginning, stating your opinion clearly, developing your opinion with details and examples, and appealing to your readers with language and emotional appeal. Here is a short poem:

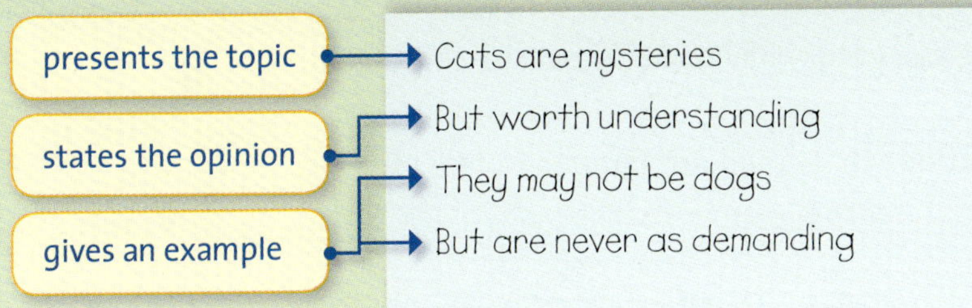

What is the grammar skill?

You will learn about **past and future tenses**.

Decoding-Spelling Connection

Some words have *silent letters* at the beginning, middle, or end of the word. These letters are silent. They are not pronounced.

My favorite season is autumn.

Lesson 24

Background and Vocabulary

Selections You Will Read

- "Chester Cricket's Pigeon Ride"
- "Central Park"

"Chester Cricket's Pigeon Ride" is **fantasy**. A fantasy

- is an imaginative story that may have unrealistic characters and events
- has events or settings that could not happen in real life
- has characters that behave in an unrealistic way

What is "Chester Cricket's Pigeon Ride" about?

This selection is about how Lulu pigeon is proud of her city and wants to show Chester Cricket some unforgettable New York City views. Feeling excitement and fear, Chester climbs aboard for a thrilling ride.

Thrilling means causing excitement and pleasure.

Roller coasters are thrilling.

What vocabulary will you learn?

Robust Vocabulary

- excursions
- pinnacle
- panic
- precious
- giddy
- gleeful
- turbulent

Tip

As you learn new words, remember to write them in your Vocabulary Log. Which words do you know very well? Which words are you still learning?

Word Bank

taxi

wilderness

brook

sycamore

Comprehension

What is the focus skill in this lesson?

The focus skill is **Literary Devices**.

Literary devices include **figurative language** that makes writing interesting and colorful. **Similes**, **metaphors**, and **personification** are all examples of figurative language.

A **simile** is a comparison using like or as. A **metaphor** is a comparison that talks about one thing as if it were another without using like or as. **Personification** is a description that gives human qualities to animals or things.

Readers can look in the text for different types of **figurative language**.

Read the passage.

Our dog Arlo looked up with his big brown eyes, asking, "Will you play with me outside? Will you?" I looked at my watch. "I have to be at school in an hour," I protested. Arlo bent his head down and stared at the floor. Suddenly he darted across the room and picked up a tennis ball. Then he looked up at me and panted, smiling with the ball in his teeth. "Well now that I found the ball we can go!" he was saying. He won.

This passage uses a the literary device of personification to help the read understand the character of the dog, Arlo, and what he means to his owner.

Grammar and Writing

What kind of writing will you do in this lesson?

You will write a **narrative composition**. You will use development through narrative elements such as characters, setting, a conflict, and a resolution. Here is a short narrative composition:

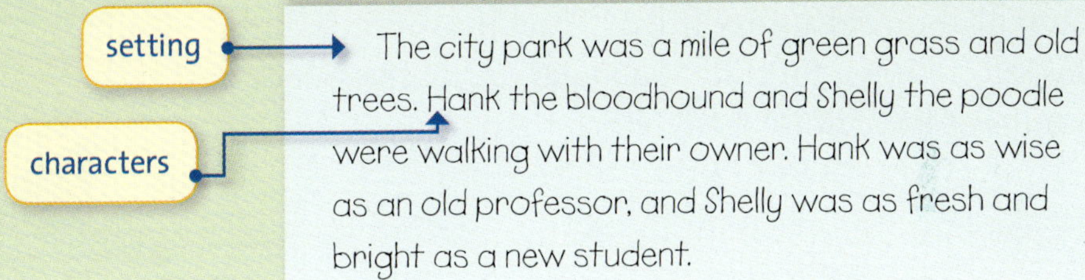

What is the grammar skill?

You will learn about **perfect tenses**.

The hawk Pale Male has flown over Central Park every day.

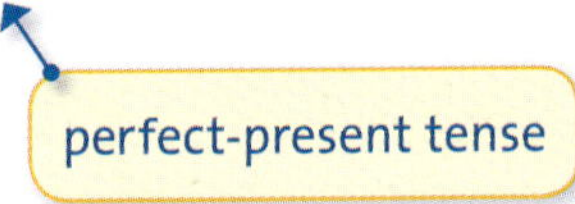

Decoding–Spelling Connection

Some words have unusual spellings in their plural forms. Changing these words from singular to plural involves more than just adding an *–s*.

country to countries

countr **–ies**

half to halves

hal **–ves**

I have cut the apples into halves. ▲

Lesson 25

Review

Background and Vocabulary

Selections You Will Read

READERS' THEATER

You will read a selection titled "The Compassion Campaign." The selection is a **Readers' Theater**.

You will also read a story titled "How Beaver Stole Fire." This selection is a **folktale**. Folktales reflect the values and customs of the culture from which they come.

COMPREHENSION STRATEGIES

What are the selections about?

"**The Compassion Campaign**" is about a television program that profiles five children who participate in community service activities.

"**How Beaver Stole Fire**" is a North American folktale about a courageous beaver who steals the secret of fire from pine trees.

beaver

What vocabulary will you learn?

Robust Vocabulary

- loathe
- bland
- mentor
- dilapidated
- coordination
- altruism
- sensibility
- advocacy
- mistreated
- compassionate

Remember to look in the Glossary for explanations of the words. What other strategies can you use?

Word Bank

Fluency

As you read "The Compassion Campaign" you will build fluency. When you read a script aloud, remember to

- read with **expression** to match your character's emotions
- adjust your **pace** to match the action in the play

Comprehension Strategies

As you read "How Beaver Stole Fire," you will review the two comprehension strategies you learned in Theme 5.

- **Summarize** Stop now and then to summarize the most important events. That will help you understand and remember what you have read.
- **Answer Questions** Use your prior knowledge and the information in the text to answer questions about what you are reading.

Writing

In Theme 5, you wrote several compositions. In Lesson 25, you will choose one of these compositions to revise. You will choose a composition to revise and publish.

Tip

Writing Traits Think about how you can use **sentence fluency** and **organization** to make your writing better.

SAMPLE REVISION

Look at how the first paragraph below was revised. What makes the revised paragraph better?

Helping others in need is a good idea. Helping others makes you feel better about yourself. I learned this lesson by helping in a day care center. I signed up to read at story time.

Ever thought about doing some volunteer work to help other people? I did, and for the first time, I felt like I could really make a difference in someone else's life. I signed up to read at story time at the local day care center. The children loved the stories, and I had a great time with them!

Lesson 26

Background and Vocabulary

Selections You Will Read

- "Lewis and Clark"
- "Hupa and Yurok Baskets"

"Lewis and Clark" is **narrative nonfiction**. **Narrative nonfiction**

- tells about people, things, events, or places that are real
- often has text features such as photographs and captions
- contains facts and important ideas about history

What is "Lewis and Clark" about?

This selection is about Lewis and Clark's exploration of the Louisiana Purchase territory.

Exploration means learning about new things through travel or study. When you explore something, you examine it carefully to find out as much as you can about it.

Expedition means a journey made to explore a new place.

Christopher Columbus was the explorer who led several expeditions to the New World.

What vocabulary will you learn?

Robust Vocabulary

- asset
- profusely
- terrain
- peril
- intently
- ordeal
- dismal
- esteem

Tip

Be a Word Detective! Look for these words in newspapers, magazines, and books. Listen for the words on the radio or television.

Word Bank

barrier

canoe

waterfall

mountain

Comprehension

What is the focus skill in this lesson?

The focus skill is **Summarize and Paraphrase**.

Summarizing and paraphrasing are related skills that help you when you read.

When you **summarize**, you restate the main ideas and most important details in a text.

When you **paraphrase**, you restate a text in your own words, without changing the meaning.

Summarizing helps readers remember the most important ideas in a text, and paraphrasing helps readers check how well they understand what they read.

Read the passage.

In the early 1800s, Lewis and Clark led an expedition to explore the Louisiana Territory. They were joined midway through their journey by an American trader and his American Indian wife, Sacagawea. The land presented the travelers with many challenges, such as crossing the Rocky Mountains. It also provided them with new information, including knowledge of over fifty American-Indian tribes.

The main points in the selection "Lewis and Clark" are combined in a brief summary. Only the most important details have been included.

Grammar and Writing

What kind of writing will you do in this lesson?

You will write a **paragraph of explanation**. You will focus on a central idea and use supporting details and examples. Here is a short paragraph of explanation:

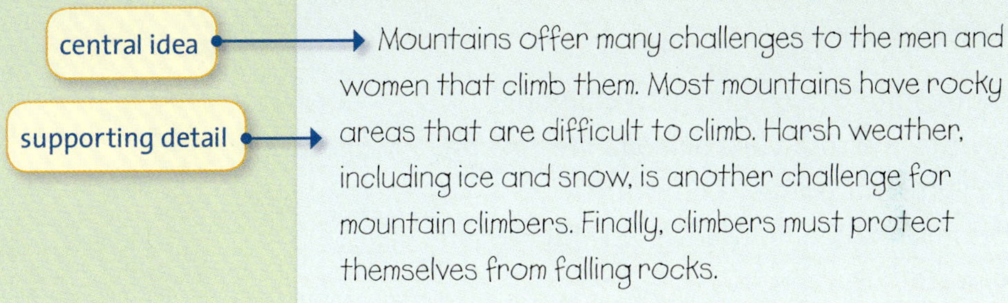

Mountains offer many challenges to the men and women that climb them. Most mountains have rocky areas that are difficult to climb. Harsh weather, including ice and snow, is another challenge for mountain climbers. Finally, climbers must protect themselves from falling rocks.

What is the grammar skill?

You will learn about **irregular verbs** and principal parts of verbs.

The explorers made exciting discoveries.

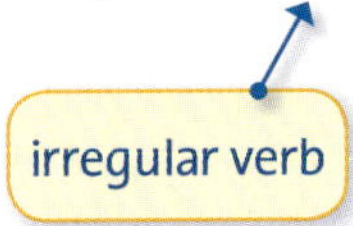

Decoding–Spelling Connection

Sometimes words are made up of a prefix, root, and suffix.

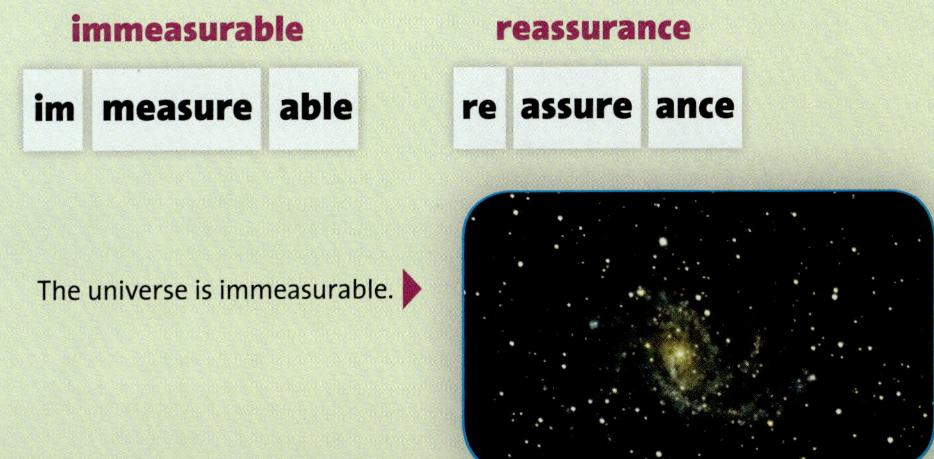

The universe is immeasurable.

Lesson 27

Background and Vocabulary

Selections You Will Read

- "Klondike Kate"
- "Sour Dough"

"Klondike Kate" is a **biography**. A biography

- is a written account of a person's life, told by someone else
- often presents events in time order
- gives information that shows why the person's life is important

What is "Klondike Kate" about?

This selection is about Kate Ryan, who travels alone to the Alaskan frontier at a time when it is unusual for women to do so. Kate endures hardships and makes a home and a name for herself in the remote Klondike.

Civilization means people living together in cities or villages.

Frontier means unexplored land where there are not yet cities or villages.

What vocabulary will you learn?

Robust Vocabulary

- remote
- appalled
- floundered
- isolated
- laden
- invest
- grueling

Tip Remember to look in the glossary for explanations of the words. What other strategies can you use?

Word Bank

Comprehension

What is the focus skill in this lesson?

The focus skill is **Summarize and Paraphrase**.

When you **summarize**, you briefly state the main ideas and most important details in a text. When you **paraphrase**, you tell a text in your own words, without changing its meaning. A **summary** should be short. A **paraphrase** can be about the same length as the original.

Read the passage.

One summer morning in the late 1800s, a young nurse named Kate Ryan was on her way to work in Vancouver, Canada. She stopped to listen when she heard a newsboy announce that gold had been discovered in the Yukon. Apparently, Skookum Jim, a Tagish Indian, had found pieces of gold as he was drinking water from his hat. After that, he and his partners discovered more gold pieces using a frying pan.

This is a **paraphrase** of the second paragraph of the selection "Klondike Kate."

Grammar and Writing

What kind of writing will you do in this lesson?

You will write a **paragraph of historical information**. You will focus each sentence of your paragraph on a single event in history. Here is a short paragraph of historical information:

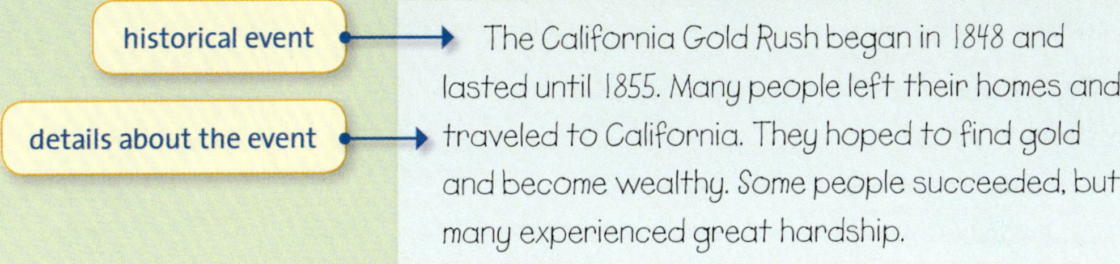

The California Gold Rush began in 1848 and lasted until 1855. Many people left their homes and traveled to California. They hoped to find gold and become wealthy. Some people succeeded, but many experienced great hardship.

What is the grammar skill?

You will learn about **contractions**.

We're reading about Alaska.

Decoding–Spelling Connection

Greek word parts include *aster/astro* (star), *chron/chrono* (time), *cycl/cyclo* (wheel), *hydr/hydro* (water), and *opt/opti* (eye).

astronomy

astro | **nomy**

hydrant

hydr | **ant**

A hydrant supplies water to firefighters.

Lesson 28

Background and Vocabulary

Selections You Will Read

- "The Top of the World"
- "On Top of the World"

"The Top of the World" is **expository nonfiction**.

Expository nonfiction

- tells about real people, places, or events
- often uses vivid words and details to describe a place
- provides facts and information about people's experiences

What is "The Top of the World" about?

This selection is about what it would be like to climb from the base of Mount Everest to its summit, the highest point on Earth.

Adventure means an unusual and exciting experience.

Danger means the risk of being hurt.

Skydiving is an exciting adventure, but it is dangerous too.

What vocabulary will you learn?

Robust Vocabulary

- summit
- accustomed
- secure
- essential
- streamlined
- acclimate

Tip

Be a Word Detective! Look for these words in newspapers, magazines, and books. Listen for the words on the radio or television.

Word Bank

Comprehension

What is the focus skill in this lesson?

The focus skill is **Fact and Opinion**.
Authors of **nonfiction** may present both facts and opinions.

A **fact** is information that can be proved to be true.

An **opinion** expresses a feeling or belief about something.

You can use an encyclopedia, an almanac, a textbook, a graphic aid, or an online source to find out if a statement is a fact.

Read the passage.

The plant life of the Alps is particularly interesting. As the mountains' height increases and the climate becomes colder, trees such as the oak, beech, and maple stop growing. Above these trees, there are short pines, and higher yet, very short shrubs. Finally, near the tops of the mountains, there are flowering plants including the glacier buttercup.

The **author's opinion** is that the plant life of the Alps is interesting. The passage also gives many facts about plant life in the Alps.

Grammar and Writing

What kind of writing will you do in this lesson?

You will write a **how-to paragraph**. You will follow the conventions of English to explain how to do something. Here is a short how-to paragraph:

instructions

sentences are complete

capitalization and punctuation are correct

Washing your hands properly is important for good health. First, make sure the water is warm. Then, using soap, rub your hands together under the water for 10 to 15 seconds. Finally, rinse your hands, and dry them with a clean towel.

What is the grammar skill?

You will learn about **adverbs**.

The children climbed carefully.

Decoding–Spelling Connection

Latin word parts include *tract* (pull or draw), *rupt* (break), *aud* (hear), and *dict* (speak or say).

tractor

tract | **or**

auditorium

aud | **itorium**

This tractor will pull a plough.

Lesson 29

Background and Vocabulary

Selections You Will Read

- "The Man Who Went to the Far Side of the Moon"
- "The Space Race"

"The Man Who Went to the Far Side of the Moon" is a biography. A **biography**

- is a written account of a person's life, told by someone else
- may include opinions and personal judgments based on facts
- presents events in time order

What is "The Man Who Went to the Far Side of the Moon" about?

This selection is about the one crew member who did not set foot on the moon's surface during the first moon walk.

Distance means being far away from another person or place.

Isolation means being separate or alone.

An adventure that takes you far away on your own can involve distance and isolation.

What vocabulary will you learn?

Robust Vocabulary

- ignited
- potentially
- squinting
- tranquility
- cramped
- jettisoned

Tip

Be a Word Detective! Look for these words in newspapers, magazines, and books. Listen for the words on the radio or television.

Word Bank

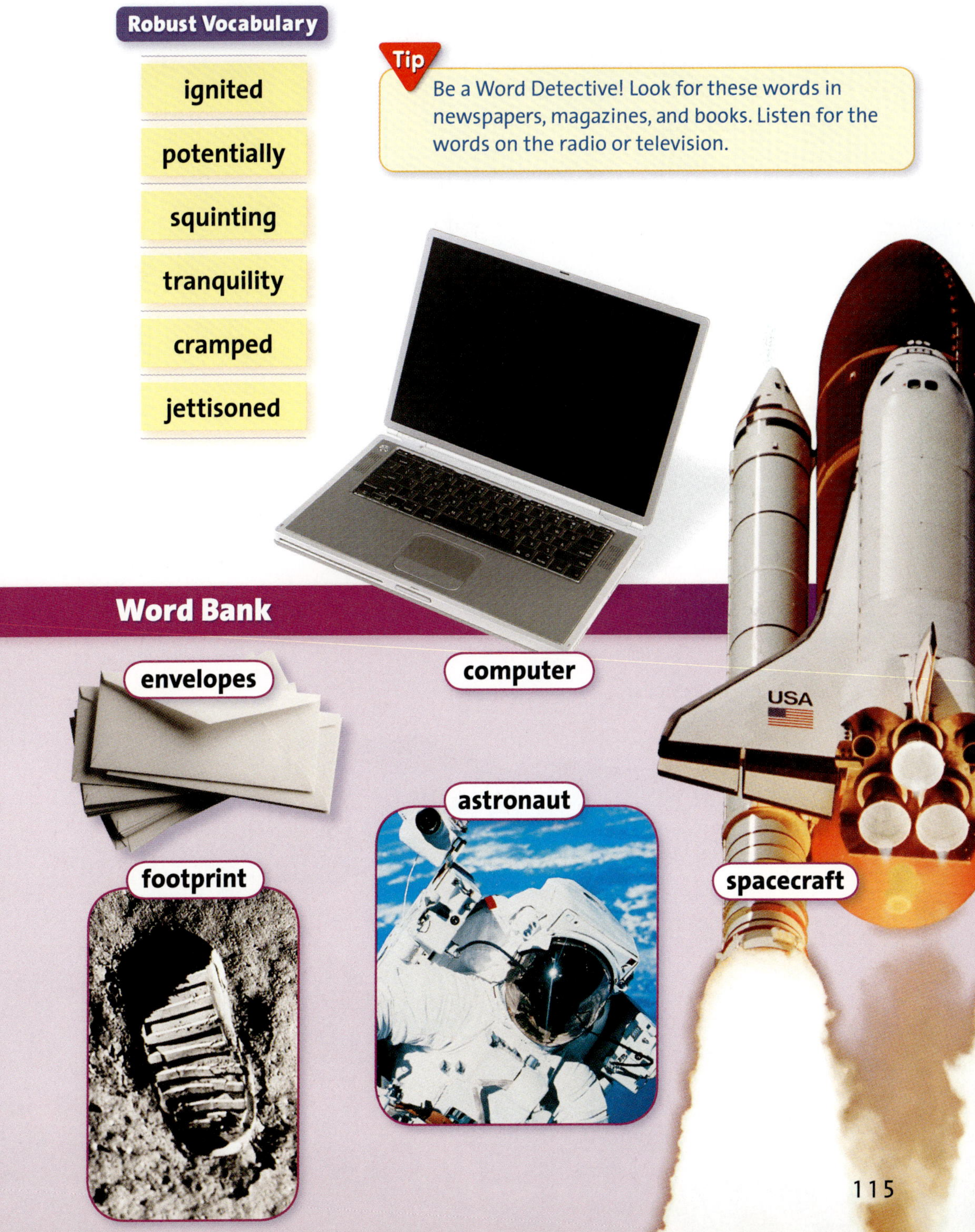

Comprehension

What is the focus skill in this lesson?

The focus skill is **Fact and Opinion**.
Authors of **nonfiction** may present both facts and opinions.

A **fact** is information or a statement that can be proved to be true

An **opinion** expresses a feeling or belief about something.

You can use an encyclopedia, an almanac, a textbook, a graphic aid, or an online source to find out if a statement is a true fact.

Read the passage.

Luna 2 was the first spacecraft to land on the moon. It was sent by the Soviet Union in 1959 as part of its space program. Luna 2 reached the moon's surface ten years before the astronauts of Apollo 11 walked there. Although the Apollo 11 mission was the most important space flight in history, Luna 2 was extremely important as well.

The first three sentences are facts. They are followed by the author's opinion in the last sentence.

Grammar and Writing

What kind of writing will you do in this lesson?

You will write an **explanatory essay**. You will follow the conventions of English to explain a topic you know well. Here is a short explanatory essay:

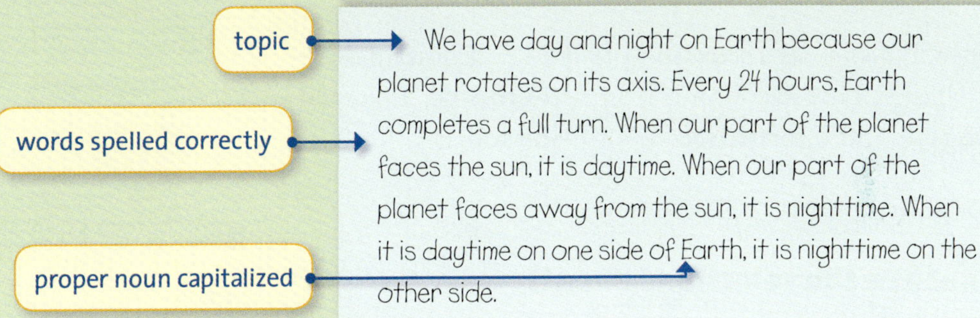

What is the grammar skill?

You will learn about **punctuation**.

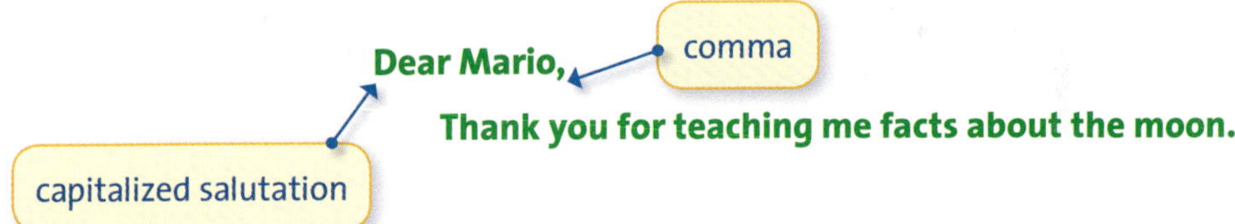

Decoding–Spelling Connection

Some English words are "borrowed" from other languages. You can use a dictionary to find out which language each word comes from.

banana
from Portuguese

The banana is a delicious fruit.

balcony
from Italian

Lesson 30

Review

Background and Vocabulary

Selections You Will Read

READERS' THEATER

You will read a selection titled "Exploring the Gulf Coast." The selection is a **Readers' Theater**.

COMPREHENSION STRATEGIES

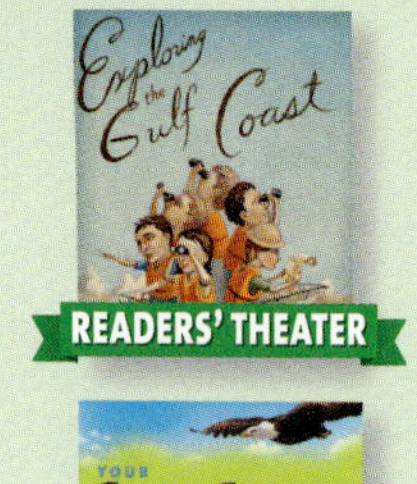

You will also read a selection titled "The Louisiana Purchase." This selection is from a **textbook**. Textbooks give facts and information about many topics.

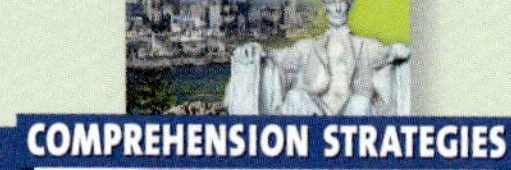

What are the selections about?

"**Exploring the Gulf Coast**" is about a photographer and four explorers who learn about Florida's Gulf Coast when they go boating with Captain Carolyn.

"**The Louisiana Purchase**" is about the importance of President Jefferson's purchase and the scope of Lewis and Clark's expedition.

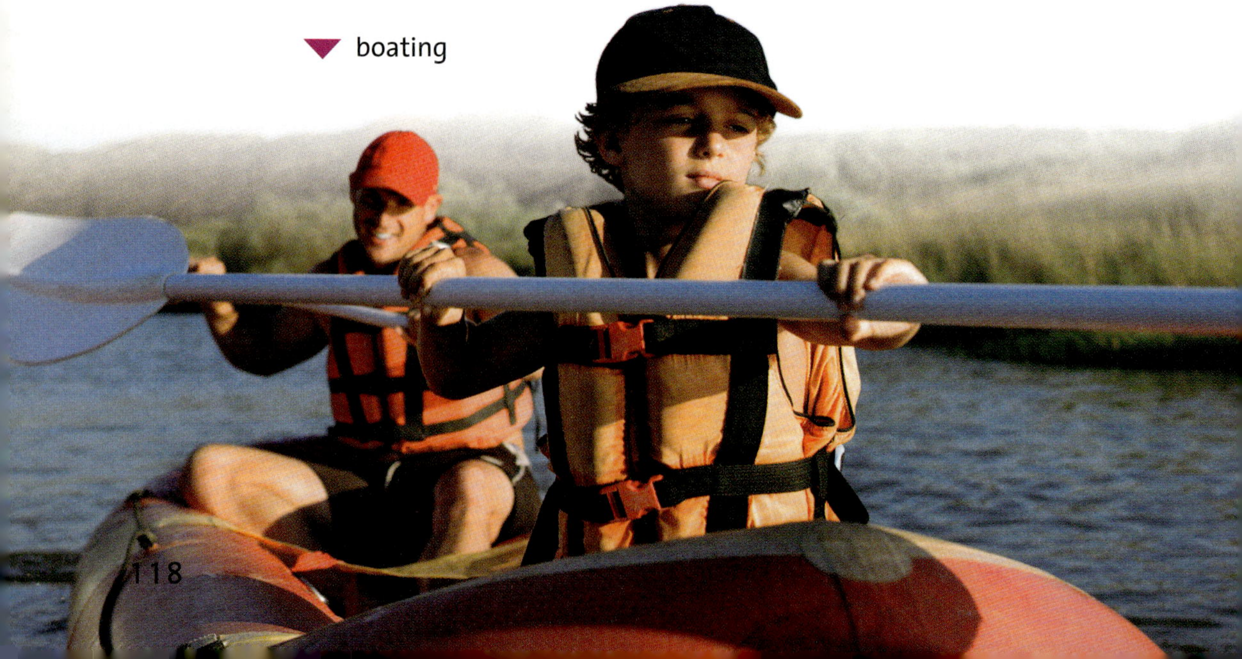

▼ boating

What vocabulary will you learn?

Robust Vocabulary

- poised
- earnestly
- insufficient
- exceptional
- achievement
- bickering
- equivalent
- regal
- customary
- provoke

Remember to look in the Glossary for explanations of the words. What other strategies can you use?

Word Bank

wolves

captain

photographer

magazines

island

Fluency

As you read "Exploring the Gulf Coast" you will build fluency. When reading a script aloud, remember to

- read with **accuracy**, pronouncing every word correctly
- pay attention to **phrasing** by pausing between groups of words that go together

Comprehension Strategies

As you read "The Louisiana Purchase," you will review the two comprehension strategies you learned in Theme 6.

- **Monitor Comprehension: Read Ahead** It is important to monitor your comprehension as you read. If you don't understand something, read ahead to find an explanation.
- **Summarize** Summarize main ideas and important details to help you remember what you read.

Writing

In Theme 6, you wrote several compositions. In Lesson 30, you will choose one of these compositions to revise. You will choose a composition to revise and publish.

Tip **Writing Traits** Think about how you can use **ideas** and **conventions** to make your writing better.

SAMPLE REVISION

Look at how the first paragraph below was revised. What makes the revised paragraph better?

Before Cassandra explored new york city, she prepared. Exploring new places is fun. she learned as much as she could about the city. she read books and looked at maps. Her friend Lauren visited Chicago last week.

Before Cassandra explored New York City, she prepared. She learned as much as she could about the city. She read books and looked at maps. She also looked at websites about New York City on the Internet.

Using the Glossary

Like a dictionary, this glossary lists words in alphabetical order. To find a word, look it up by its first letter or letters.

To save time, use the **guide words** at the top of each page. These show you the first and last words on the page. Look at the guide words to see if your word falls between them alphabetically.

Here is an example of a glossary entry:

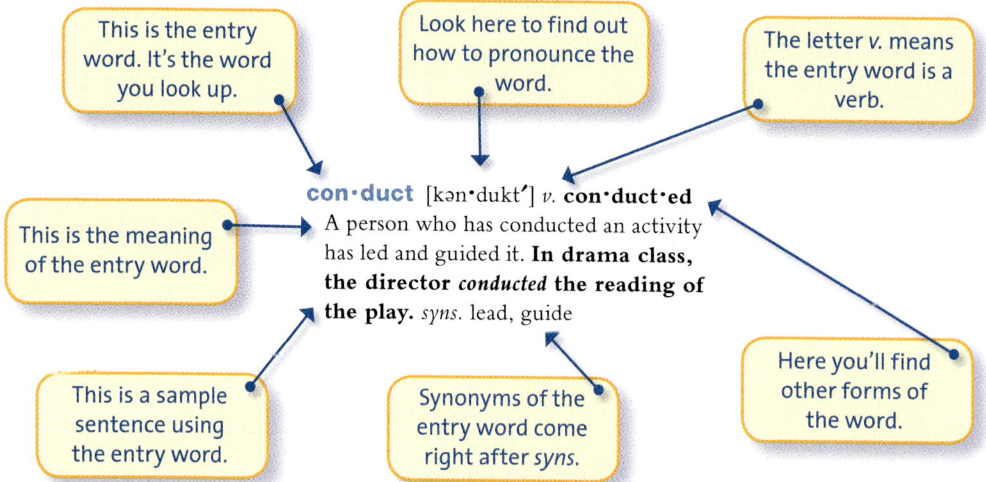

Word Origins

Throughout the glossary, you will find notes about word origins, or how words came into use and have changed over time. Words often have interesting backgrounds that can help you remember what they mean. Here is an example of a word origin note:

> **Word Origins**
>
> **charity** The origin of *charity* is the Latin word *carus*, which means "dear" and "love." In the Middle Ages, *carus* became *cherite* and *charite*, meaning "love of other people" and "kindness."

Pronunciation

The pronunciation in brackets is a respelling that shows how the word is pronounced. The **pronunciation key** explains what the symbols in a respelling mean. A shortened pronunciation key appears on every other page of the glossary.

PRONUNCIATION KEY

a	add, map	m	move, seem	u	up, done
ā	ace, rate	n	nice, tin	û(r)	burn, term
â(r)	care, air	ng	ring, song	yo͞o	fuse, few
ä	palm, father	o	odd, hot	v	vain, eve
b	bat, rub	ō	open, so	w	win, away
ch	check, catch	ô	order, jaw	y	yet, yearn
d	dog, rod	oi	oil, boy	z	zest, muse
e	end, pet	ou	pout, now	zh	vision, pleasure
ē	equal, tree	o͝o	took, full	ə	the schwa, an
f	fit, half	o͞o	pool, food		unstressed vowel
g	go, log	p	pit, stop		representing the
h	hope, hate	r	run, poor		sound spelled
i	it, give	s	see, pass		*a* in *above*
ī	ice, write	sh	sure, rush		*e* in *sicken*
j	joy, ledge	t	talk, sit		*i* in *possible*
k	cool, take	th	thin, both		*o* in *melon*
l	look, rule	t̶h̶	this, bathe		*u* in *circus*

Other symbols:

· separates words into syllables

ˈ indicates heavier stress on a syllable

ˌ indicates lighter stress on a syllable

Abbreviations: ***adj.*** **adjective,** ***adv.*** **adverb,** ***conj.*** **conjunction,** ***interj.*** **interjection,** ***n.*** **noun,** ***prep.*** **preposition,** ***pron.*** **pronoun,** ***syn.*** **synonym,** ***v.*** **verb**

A

ab·sent·mind·ed [ab′sənt·mīn′did] *adj.* Someone who is absentminded forgets things easily. **Naomi thought Pedro was *absentminded* because he forgot to order food for the party.** *syn.* forgetful

ac·cli·mate [ak′lə·māt] *v.* If you acclimate to something, you adjust to a new condition or environment. **The goldfish had to *acclimate* to the larger tank.** *syns.* adapt, adjust

acclimate

ac·cu·mu·late [ə·kyōōm′yə·lāt] *v.* When things accumulate, they collect over time. **When I noticed the newspapers *accumulate* in front of Mr. Smith's house, I realized he was probably out of town again.** *syn.* pile up

FACT FILE

accumulate Literally, *accumulate* means "to heap up." This meaning is reflected in the name *cumulus* clouds for the big, fluffy clouds that heap up in the sky.

ACADEMIC LANGUAGE

accuracy When you read with *accuracy*, you read without making mistakes.

ac·cus·tomed [ə·kus′təmd] *adj.* If you are accustomed to something, you are used to it because it has been a regular part of your life. **Charlie became *accustomed* to eating cereal for a snack.** *syn.* acclimated

a·chieve·ment [ə·chēv′mənt] *n.* An achievement is the result of a successful effort. **Janice was proud of her *achievement* as winner of the spelling bee.** *syns.* accomplishment, success

ad·just [ə·just′] *v.* When you adjust, you change your behavior to fit a new situation. **When the cat moved from the shelter to a home with three small children, it had to *adjust* to its new environment.** *syn.* modify

ad·vo·ca·cy [ad′və·kə·sē] *n.* Advocacy is giving support to a person, idea, or cause. **Amar showed his *advocacy* for stray animals by asking his parents if he could adopt a dog from the Humane Society.** *syns.* support, backing

a·ghast [ə·gast′] *adj.* If you are aghast, you feel shocked and disgusted about something. **Keisha was *aghast* at her friend's rude behavior.** *syn.* appalled

al·tru·ism [al′trōō·iz·əm] *n.* Altruism is being concerned about others before worrying about oneself. **David showed that *altruism* was part of his nature when he volunteered to read to children at the day-care center.** *syn.* kindness

a·mend [ə·mend′] *v.* **a·mends** When you amend something, you make positive changes, such as amending a shopping list or a recipe. **After forgetting to invite Xenia to her party, Aylana *amends* her mistake by inviting Xenia to a sleepover.** *syn.* correct

an·a·lyze [an′ə·līz] *v.* **an·a·lyz·ing** A scientist who is analyzing something is studying it closely to figure out how it works or what it is made of. **The scientist in the laboratory is *analyzing* the water to make sure it is safe to drink.** *syn.* examine

ap·pall [ə·pôl′] *v.* **ap·palled** Someone who is appalled is shocked and horrified at something. **After the storm, Mercedes was *appalled* to find that a tree had fallen on the roof of her house.** *syn.* dismay

Word Origins

appall The word *appall* traces its roots back to the French word *apallir,* which means "to become or make pale." It was not used to mean "shock and dismay" until the nineteenth century.

ap·peal [ə·pēl′] *v.* **ap·pealed** If you have appealed to someone, you have made a request with a lot of feeling. **Alejandro *appealed* to Ramona's good nature when he begged her to help him study for the math test.** *syn.* plead

ap·pro·pri·ate [ə·prō′prē·it] *adj.* If you wear appropriate clothing, you choose an outfit that is right for the situation. **Dwayne felt that a suit and tie would be the *appropriate* attire for the award ceremony.** *syn.* suitable

as·set [as′et] *n.* An asset is a resource, person, or object that is valuable to have. **My mother says her most valuable *asset* is her family.** *syn.* resource

as·suage [ə·swāj′] *v.* To assuage guilt is to make it less painful and troubling. **To *assuage* his bad feelings about spilling ketchup on his father's best shirt, Dan mowed the lawn.** *syn.* pacify

as·sure [ə·sho͝or′] *v.* **as·sured** If someone has assured you of something, he or she has said words to make you feel positive that things will be all right. **My older brother *assured* me that he had changed the flat tire and that it was safe to continue our trip.** *syn.* guarantee

ACADEMIC LANGUAGE

autobiography An *autobiography* is the story of a real person's life written by that person.

B

baf·fled [baf′əld] *adj.* Someone who is baffled by something cannot understand or explain it. **Emiko was *baffled* when she saw that her mother had sent cookies and candy, instead of the usual sandwich, for lunch.** *syn.* puzzled

bask [bask] *v.* **bask·ing** If an animal is basking, it is exposing itself to warmth in the sun. **Miguel was *basking* in the backyard on the lawn chair.** *syn.* sunbathe

bel·low·ing [bel′ō·ing] *adj.* A bellowing sound is a loud, low-pitched sound, usually made to show distress. **My dog makes *bellowing* sounds when he goes to the veterinarian.** *syn.* crying

be·tray [bi·trā′] *v.* **be·trayed** If you betrayed someone who trusted you, you gave away his or her plans, ideas, or secrets to others. **Megan said I had *betrayed* her when I told Stephanie her secret.** *syn.* double-cross

a add	e end	o odd	o͞o pool	oi oil	th this	ə = *a* in *above*
ā ace	ē equal	ō open	u up	ou pout	zh vision	*e* in *sicken*
â care	i it	ô order	û burn	ng ring		*i* in *possible*
ä palm	ī ice	o͝o took	yo͞o fuse	th thin		*o* in *melon*
						u in *circus*

bick·er [bik'ər] *v.* **bick·er·ing** People who are bickering are arguing about something unimportant. **Jeff and Hilda are *bickering* about who gets the window seat on the plane ride.** *syn.* argue

ACADEMIC LANGUAGE

biography A *biography* is the story of a real person's life written by another person.

bland [bland] *adj.* Something that is bland is dull and unexciting. **Aunt Elena's chicken casserole was *bland* because she had forgotten to add salt and pepper.** *syn.* flavorless

bois·ter·ous [bois'tər·əs *or* bois'trəs] *adj.* A boisterous person or animal is noisy and has lots of energy. **The *boisterous* new puppy was constantly jumping on the furniture.** *syn.* rowdy

brim [brim] *v.* **brim·ming** Something that is brimming is filled to the very top. **Liang was thirsty, so he filled his cup until it was *brimming* with juice.** *syn.* full

brimming

broach [brōch] *v.* **broached** A ship that has broached is in danger of sinking because it has veered so that the waves strike its side. **I saw a movie in which a ship *broached* and objects were falling overboard.** *syn.* capsize

bus·tle [bus'əl] *v.* **bus·tles** When someone bustles, he or she moves in a busy, energetic way. **When my mother has guests for dinner, she *bustles* about the kitchen making sure the food is correctly prepared.** *syn.* dart

C

char·i·ty [char'ə·tē] *n.* Charity is showing kindness by giving money or gifts to organizations that need them. **She shows *charity* by giving some of her allowance to the Animal Rescue League.** *syn.* goodwill

Word Origins

charity The origin of *charity* is the Latin word *carus*, which means "dear" and "love." In the Middle Ages, *carus* became *cherite* and *charite*, meaning "love of other people" and "kindness."

cir·cu·late [sûr'kyə·lāt] *v.* When you circulate, you move freely around an area. **When the doorbell rang, Susan had just begun to *circulate* among the guests at her party.** *syn.* wander

coax [kōks] *v.* **coaxed** If you are coaxed into doing something, you are gently talked into it by someone else. **Akedo *coaxed* Aretha into jogging with him, even though she doesn't like outdoor exercise.** *syn.* persuade

com·part·ment [kəm·pärt'mənt] *n.* **com·part·ments** An item that has compartments has separate sections for keeping things. **My craft box has many *compartments,* in which I store items such as crayons, markers, and brushes.** *syn.* section

compartment

com·pas·sion·ate [kəm·pash′ən·it] *adj.* A compassionate person is kindhearted and understanding. **Isabel showed that she was *compassionate* by inviting the new girl to eat lunch with her.** *syn.* kind

con·ceit·ed [kən·sē′tid] *adj.* A conceited person thinks too highly of herself or himself. **Michael's announcement that he is the most well-liked student in the school shows how *conceited* he is.** *syn.* arrogant

con·coc·tion [kən·kok′shən] *n.* A concoction is a mix of different things, often one put together without much planning. **In science class, we put together a *concoction* of white glue, food coloring, and rock salt to make objects that represented precious stones.** *syn.* mixture

con·duct [kən·dukt′] *v.* **con·duct·ed** A person who has conducted an activity has led and guided it. **In drama class, the director *conducted* the reading of the play.** *syn.* direct

ACADEMIC LANGUAGE

conventions A *convention* is an agreement about what is correct in usage or custom. Conventions of the English language include the rules of grammar, spelling, punctuation, and capitalization.

co·or·di·na·tion [kō·ôr′də·nā′shən] *n.* Coordination involves organizing the different parts of something so that they work well together. **The sports award assembly was successful thanks to the *coordination* by Marshall.** *syn.* management

cramped [krampt] *adj.* A place that is cramped is uncomfortable because there is very little free space. **Sitting around the dinner table gets especially *cramped* when Aunt Sylvia and Uncle Harry bring their children to visit.** *syn.* crowded

cri·sis [krī′səs] *n.* A crisis is a situation that suddenly becomes very dangerous or difficult. **Chita smelled smoke and immediately knew a *crisis* existed in her apartment building.** *syn.* emergency

cru·cial [kro͞o′shəl] *adj.* If something is crucial, it is extremely important. **Manuel's mother and father made a *crucial* decision to move to another state.** *syn.* important

cru·sade [kro͞o·sād′] *v.* **cru·sad·ed** A person who has crusaded has worked hard to make a change based on his or her beliefs. **Pam's parents *crusaded* for her school to include an art program and a music program as part of the curriculum.** *syn.* campaign

cum·ber·some [kum′bər·səm] *adj.* Something that is cumbersome is large, heavy, and difficult to handle. **My suitcase was too *cumbersome* to lift into the overhead compartment, so I put it under my seat.** *syn.* unwieldy

cus·tom·ar·y [kus′tə·mâr′ē] *adj.* Something that is customary is what is usual or normal. **In the spring, it is *customary* for Sergio and his friends to play baseball in the park.** *syn.* usual

a	add	e	end	o	odd	o͞o	pool	oi	oil	th	this
ā	ace	ē	equal	ō	open	u	up	ou	pout	zh	vision
â	care	i	it	ô	order	û	burn	ng	ring		
ä	palm	ī	ice	o͝o	took	yo͞o	fuse	th	thin		

ə = *a* in *above*, *e* in *sicken*, *i* in *possible*, *o* in *melon*, *u* in *circus*

D

dam·age [dam′ij] *v.* If you damage something, you harm or injure it. **A hurricane can *damage* the electrical system of an entire region.** *syn.* harm

de·bris [də·brē′] *n.* Debris is scattered pieces of something that has been destroyed. **The tornado turned our storage shed into a trail of *debris*.** *syn.* rubble

FACT FILE

debris The word *debris* comes from the French word *débriser,* which means "to break down or crush." Nearly thirty percent of the words in the English language have a French origin.

de·duc·tion [di·duk′shən] *n.* A deduction is a conclusion you reach, based on the information you have been given. **Tomás read the buyer's guide and made the *deduction* that the more expensive bicycle was the better choice.** *syn.* conclusion

de·flate [di·flāt′] *v.* **de·flat·ed** If someone feels deflated, he or she has lost confidence about something. **Janice felt *deflated* and unsure of her baking abilities after she lost the cookie-baking contest.** *syn.* drain

des·ig·nat·ed [dez′ig·nāt·ed] *adj.* If a place is designated, it is chosen for a special purpose. **The bookstore was the *designated* meeting place for Guillermo and George.** *syn.* assigned

des·o·late [des′ə·lit] *adj.* A person who feels desolate feels lonely and sad. **Jenny felt *desolate* after all her friends went out of town for the summer.** *syn.* lonely

des·per·ate·ly [des′pər·it·lē] *adv.* Wanting something desperately means wanting it so much that you'll do almost anything to get it. **Darnel *desperately* wants to become a famous writer and the author of best-selling books.** *syn.* greatly

des·ti·ny [des′tə·nē] *n.* To believe in destiny is to feel that certain things will happen because they were meant to be. **When Toshi found a violin in the attic, he felt it was his *destiny* to enter music school.** *syn.* fate

de·tect [di·tekt′] *v.* When you detect something, you notice or discover it. **She would be a good computer technician because she can *detect* and repair problems in computer hardware.** *syns.* discover, notice

de·vice [di·vīs′] *n.* A device is an object that has been made for a special purpose. **Tony's aunt wears a hearing aid, a *device* that helps people with hearing loss.** *syn.* tool

dig·ni·fied [dig′nə·fīd] *adj.* To act in a dignified way means to behave in a calm, serious, and respectful manner. **Everyone behaved in a *dignified* manner during the meeting.** *syn.* respectful

dignified

di·lap·i·dat·ed [di·lap′ə·dā·təd] *adj.* A dilapidated building looks worn out and run down. **After the neighbors complained that the *dilapidated* house was dangerous, the owner made repairs to make the place safe.** *syns.* run down, decayed

dis·grun·tled [dis·grun′təld] *adj.* If you are disgruntled, you are unhappy because things have not turned out the way you wanted. **The worker was *disgruntled* and wanted a better job.** *syn.* unhappy

dis·heart·ened [dis·här′tənd] *adj.* If you are disheartened, you feel disappointed and less hopeful. **Lisa wants to be an actor, so she was *disheartened* that she didn't get a part in the movie.** *syn.* disappointed

dis·mal [diz′məl] *adj.* Something that is dismal is bleak and depressing. **The constant rain made April a *dismal* month.** *syn.* gloomy

> **Word Origins**
>
> **dismal** In medieval times, certain days were thought to be unlucky. These days were said to be *dies mali,* which in Latin means "bad days." Over the years, *dies mali* came into English as *dismal* and means "gloomy."

dis·may [dis·mā′] *v.* **dis·mayed** When you are dismayed, you are upset about something and unsure of how to deal with it. **Eduardo's sisters were *dismayed* when he refused to let them ride on his new bike.** *syn.* upset

dra·mat·i·cal·ly [drə·mat′i·klē] *adv.* If something is done dramatically, it is done in a striking or impressive way. **Connie *dramatically* and excitedly told about seeing a bear while camping with her family in a national park.** *syns.* vividly, spectacularly

dwell [dwel] *v.* The place where you dwell is where you live. **I think it might be hard to *dwell* in an igloo for a long time.** *syns.* reside, inhabit

E

ear·nest·ly [ûr′nist·lē] *adv.* Someone who speaks earnestly says things in an especially serious and honest way. **In his report about the environment, Terrel *earnestly* expressed his views.** *syn.* candidly

ec·cen·tric [ik·sen′trik] *adj.* An eccentric person has habits or opinions that seem odd to other people. **Everyone thinks Akemi is *eccentric* because she walks backward up flights of stairs.** *syns.* odd, unusual

> **Word Origins**
>
> **eccentric** The word *eccentric* comes from the Greek word *ékkentros,* which means "out of the center." It wasn't until the early 1800s that the term *eccentric* was used to describe a person who seemed odd or unusual.

e·las·tic [i·las′tik] *adj.* Something that is elastic stretches easily. **These shorts have an *elastic* waistband.** *syn.* flexible

> **FACT FILE**
>
> **elastic** If something is *elastic,* it might be made of rubber. Natural rubber comes from the juice of fig-like trees that grow in areas near the equator.

e·lon·gate [i·lông′gāt] *v.* **e·lon·gates** Something that elongates stretches to a longer length. **Mark *elongates* the clay pieces he uses for the hair of his sculpture.** *syns.* lengthen, extend

a	add	e	end	o	odd	o͞o	pool	oi	oil	th	this
ā	ace	ē	equal	ō	open	u	up	ou	pout	zh	vision
â	care	i	it	ô	order	û	burn	ng	ring		
ä	palm	ī	ice	o͝o	took	yo͞o	fuse	th	thin		

ə = *a* in *above*, *e* in *sicken*, *i* in *possible*, *o* in *melon*, *u* in *circus*

em·bark [im·bärk′] *v.* **em·barked** If you have embarked on a journey, you have begun a new adventure. **After Lana packed her gear, she *embarked* on her trip to the mountains.** *syn.* start

em·i·nent [em′ə·nənt] *adj.* An eminent person is well known and important. **The *eminent* doctor developed a number of procedures for saving lives.** *syns.* renowned, famous

en·coun·ter [in·koun′tər] *v.* **en·coun·tered** If you encountered someone, you met that person unexpectedly. **Shuko was very surprised when he *encountered* his father in the fast-food restaurant.** *syn.* meet

en·deav·or [in·dev′ər] *n.* An endeavor is an activity or task you take on in an effort to accomplish it. **In her *endeavor* to raise money for band uniforms, Rosario organized a car wash.** *syn.* effort

en·rap·ture [in·rap′chər] *v.* **en·rap·tured** A person who is enraptured is delighted and thrilled with something. **The students planted a garden and were *enraptured* when they saw the flowers bloom.** *syn.* enchant

en·ter·pris·ing [en′tər·prīz·ing] *adj.* People who are enterprising do new and difficult things in order to achieve their goals. **Andrew took the *enterprising* step of opening an art gallery at the school.** *syn.* adventurous

en·vi·sion [in·vizh′ən] *v.* **en·vi·sioned** If you have pictured something in your mind, you have envisioned it. **Reneé *envisioned* herself arriving at a castle on a winged horse.** *syn.* visualize

e·quiv·a·lent [i·kwiv′ə·lənt] *adj.* Things that are equivalent are equal. **My twin sister and I received *equivalent* gifts at our birthday party.** *syn.* alike

es·ca·pade [es′kə·pād] *n.* **es·ca·pades** Escapades are carefree, mischievous, or reckless adventures. **Carmen and Gabriella play board games for fun and never go on *escapades*.** *syn.* adventure

es·sence [es′əns] *n.* The essence of something is its most basic, important quality. **The *essence* of being a mathematician is being able to work well with numbers.** *syn.* core

es·sen·tial [i·sen′shəl] *adj.* Something that is essential is absolutely necessary. **Jerome knew that it was *essential* to study in order to pass the test.** *syns.* necessary, crucial

es·teem [i·stēm′] *v.* To esteem something means to judge it to be of value. **I *esteem* it an honor to be elected to student council.** *syns.* regard, value

ex·cep·tion·al [ik·sep′shən·əl] *adj.* Something that is exceptional is special, and it stands above others like it. **Ramón's *exceptional* character showed when he decided to volunteer at the senior citizen center.** *syn.* extraordinary

ex·cur·sion [ik·skûr′zhən] *n.* **ex·cur·sions** An excursion is a short journey or outing. **Melanie's family went on an *excursion* down the river.** *syn.* outing

excursion

ex·hil·a·rate [ig·zil′ə·rāt′e] *v.* **ex·hil·a·rat·ed** If you feel exhilarated, you feel very excited and energetic. **Ryan was *exhilarated* to learn that he placed first in the swimming competition.** *syns.* excite, thrill

ex·pec·ta·tion [ek·spek·tā′shən] *n.* **ex·pec·ta·tions** Expectations are hopes about how well others will do or about how they should behave. **Wilma's parents have *expectations* that she will be on her best behavior at summer camp.** *syns.* hope, belief

ACADEMIC LANGUAGE

expository nonfiction *Expository nonfiction* presents and explains facts about a topic. Photographs, captions, and headings are commonly found in these texts.

expression Reading aloud with *expression* means using your voice to match the action of the story and the characters' feelings.

ex·trav·a·gant [ik·strav′ə·gənt] *adj.* Something extravagant is much more costly or elaborate than what is really needed. **Nina thought the *extravagant* ring was beautiful.** *syn.* excessive

extravagant

F

ACADEMIC LANGUAGE

fable A *fable* is a short story that teaches a lesson or moral about life. Fables often include animals as characters.

fantasy A *fantasy* is an imaginative story that may have unrealistic characters and events.

faze [fāz] *v.* If things faze you, they bother or confuse you. **Even though Steve wanted to make the chess team, it didn't *faze* him that the tryouts were cancelled.** *syn.* daunt

feat [fēt] *n.* A feat is a difficult act that impresses people. **Climbing the highest mountain in the world is a *feat* not many people in the world can claim.** *syn.* accomplishment

fer·vor [fûr′vər] *n.* A person who speaks with fervor speaks with great emotion and strong belief. **Frances spoke to the students with *fervor* in her speech at the graduation ceremony.** *syn.* enthusiasm

fe·ver·ish·ly [fē′vər·ish·lē] *adv.* If you are working feverishly, you are working quickly and excitedly. **As the thunderstorm became more threatening, Gibran worked *feverishly* to bring the lawn furniture inside.** *syn.* busily

a add	e end	o odd	o͞o pool	oi oil	t͟h this	ə = *a* in *above*
ā ace	ē equal	ō open	u up	ou pout	zh vision	*e* in *sicken*
â care	i it	ô order	û burn	ng ring		*i* in *possible*
ä palm	ī ice	o͝o took	yo͞o fuse	th thin		*o* in *melon*
						u in *circus*

fick·le [fik′əl] *adj.* Fickle people keep changing their minds about what they like or want. **Shantell is *fickle* about her clothes because she wears her outfits a couple of times but then wants to give them away and get new ones.** *syn.* indecisive

flop [flop] *n.* A flop is a failure. **Jorge's ant farm was a *flop* at the science fair because all the ants died.** *syn.* failure

floun·der [floun′dər] *v.* **floun·dered** People or animals that have floundered have made wild movements trying to get something done. **Otis *floundered* about on the dance floor as he tried to learn the new dance step.** *syn.* blunder

ACADEMIC LANGUAGE

focus Writers *focus* on a topic by connecting every idea and detail to the topic. Fiction writers use focus to concentrate the reader's attention on a theme or story element.

folktale A *folktale* is a story that reflects the customs and beliefs of a culture. Folktales were first told orally and have been passed down through generations in a region or culture.

fret [fret] *v.* When you fret about something, you keep thinking and worrying about it. **Brad tried not to *fret* about giving his book report in front of the class.** *syn.* worry

fringe [frinj] *n.* **fring·es** The fringes of a place are areas along its edges, far away from the center of action. **In the cattle drives of the late 1800s, cattle were herded to the railroads from the *fringes* of the territory.** *syns.* border, outskirts

ACADEMIC LANGUAGE

functional text *Functional text* is writing used in everyday life, such as e-mail messages, manuals, and directions.

G

gen·ial [jēn′yəl] *adj.* A genial person is warm and friendly. **Nora welcomed her cousins in a *genial* way and invited them to stay for dinner.** *syns.* friendly, hospitable

ges·ture [jes′chər] *n.* A gesture is something you say or do in order to express a feeling to someone. **Elliot gave Sierra a new set of drumsticks as a *gesture* of welcoming her to the band.** *syn.* token

gid·dy [gid′ē] *adj.* If you feel giddy, you feel happy in a silly, dizzy way. **Tamika felt *giddy* when she got on her new bike for the first time.** *syn.* excited

glee·ful [glē′fəl] *adj.* A person who is gleeful is excited and happy, sometimes as a result of someone else's mistake. **When Abby spelled her third word correctly, she had the *gleeful* feeling that she could win the spelling bee.** *syn.* joyful

gouge [gouj] *v.* **goug·es** If someone gouges something, he or she makes a deep cut or dent in it. **Using a sharp tool, Tito's dad *gouges* a design in the wood frame.** *syn.* cut

gour·met [go͝or·mā′] *adj.* Gourmet food is food that is expensive, rare, or carefully prepared. **My father always makes a *gourmet* meal to celebrate my birthday.**

FACT FILE

gourmet The word *gourmet* came from the Old French word *grou-met*, which meant "a person who grooms horses." In time, the word came to be spelled *gourmet* and referred to any servant in a house. Over time, the name applied to servants who tasted people's food and drink for them.

grate·ful [grāt′fəl] *adj.* To be grateful is to feel thankful for someone or something. **Reggie is *grateful* that his grandparents let him spend every summer on their farm because he wants to be a farmer, too.** *syn.* appreciative

grim [grim] *adj.* If something looks grim, it appears serious and forbidding. **With their frowns and crossed arms, Joann and Debbie looked *grim*.** *syn.* dour

grim

grudg·ing·ly [gruj′ing·lē] *adv.* If you say something grudgingly, you say it without really wanting to. **Bob *grudgingly* told Frank that he could use his computer.** *syn.* reluctantly

gru·el·ing [gro͞o′əl·ing] *adj.* A grueling experience is extremely difficult and exhausting. **The jogger chose to run in the morning because working out in the afternoon heat was too *grueling*.** *syns.* demanding, exhausting

H

hes·i·tate [hez′ə·tāt] *v.* **hes·i·tat·ing** If you are hesitating, you are pausing before doing something because you are feeling unsure. **Hector is *hesitating* before entering the music contest because he is not sure he will have enough time to practice.** *syn.* vacillate

hi·a·tus [hī·ā′təs] *n.* A hiatus is a break for a period of time between events. **Miya had an unexpected *hiatus* from the basketball team when she sprained her ankle.** *syns.* break, pause

ACADEMIC LANGUAGE

historical documents *Historical documents* are papers written in the past.

historical fiction *Historical fiction* stories are set in the past and portray people, places, and events that did happen or could have happened.

a add	e end	o odd	o͞o pool	oi oil	th this	ə = *a* in *above*
ā ace	ē equal	ō open	u up	ou pout	zh vision	*e* in *sicken*
â care	i it	ô order	û burn	ng ring		*i* in *possible*
ä palm	ī ice	o͝o took	yo͞o fuse	th thin		*o* in *melon*
						u in *circus*

hu·mil·i·a·tion [hyōō·mil′ē·ā′shən] *n.* Humiliation is a feeling of shame or embarrassment. **Julio guided the new student to the right classroom to spare her the *humiliation* of arriving in class late.** *syn.* embarrassment

I

ig·nite [ig·nīt′] *v.* **ig·nit·ed** When something is ignited, it is lit or made to burn. **The workers who *ignited* the Fourth of July fireworks were trained in a special safety course.** *syn.* inflame

im·mac·u·late [i·mak′yə·lət] *adj.* Something that is immaculate is extremely clean and tidy. **Liana's house is ready for guests at any moment because she keeps it in *immaculate* shape.** *syn.* clean

im·pass·a·ble [im·pas′ə·bəl] *adj.* A road or path that is impassable is impossible to travel on. **In the winter, certain roads through the Sierra Nevada are *impassable* because of heavy snows.** *syn.* blocked

in·ad·e·quate [in·ad′ə·kwit] *adj.* Something that is inadequate is not as good or as large as it needs to be. **The number of pancakes the chef had prepared was *inadequate* for the huge breakfast crowd.** *syn.* insufficient

Word Origins

inadequate The word *inadequate* is made up of the Latin prefix *in*, which means "not" and the Latin word *adaequātus,* which means "equalized."

in·di·ca·tion [in·də·kā′shən] *n.* An indication is a sign that something exists or might happen. **The baby's crying all night was an *indication* that he was sick.** *syn.* sign

in·dig·nant·ly [in·dig′nənt·lē] *adv.* When you say something indignantly, you show irritation because you feel you have been insulted or treated unfairly. **Ira declared *indignantly* that if he couldn't sit in the front seat, he didn't want to go on the trip.** *syn.* resentfully

in·dus·try [in′dəs·trē] *n.* An industry is all the people and companies that make a certain type of product or provide a certain type of service. **The automobile *industry* puts on shows every year to introduce the new models.** *syn.* business

Word Origins

industry The origin of the word *industry* can be traced back to the Latin word *indostruus*, whose root, *struere*, means "to build." The Latin word part *indu* means "in." The word came to have its present usage in the mid-sixteenth century.

in·flam·ma·ble [in·flam′ə·bəl] *adj.* Something that is inflammable can catch fire easily and burn rapidly. **Parents should be careful not to dress their babies in pajamas that are *inflammable.*** *syn.* combustible

ACADEMIC LANGUAGE

informational narrative An *informational narrative* is a story that presents information and facts.

informational text *Informational text* presents information and facts.

in·fu·ri·ate [in·fyŏŏr′ē·āte] *v.* **in·fu·ri·at·ed** Something that infuriated you made you feel extremely angry. **Jay was *infuriated* when his brother ate the last piece of Jay's birthday cake.** *syn.* enrage

in·sight [in′sīt] *n.* **in·sights** If you have insights, you notice or understand important things that other people may not see. **The teacher seemed to have special *insights* about which of her students would make good leaders.** *syn.* perception

in·stinct [in′stingkt] *n.* An instinct is a natural, almost automatic way that people or animals react to things. **The mother bear's *instinct* was to protect her cub from other animals.** *syn.* intuition

in·suf·fi·cient [in·sə·fi′shənt] *adj.* If something is insufficient, there is not enough of it or it is not good enough to meet the need. **The two cans of paint Pat bought were an *insufficient* amount to paint the entire house.** *syn.* inadequate

in·tent·ly [in·tent′lē] *adv.* When you do something intently, you do it with great concentration. **I enjoy learning about the oceans, so I watched and listened *intently* to the documentary about global currents.** *syn.* attentively

in·ter·nal [in·tûr′nəl] *adj.* Something that is internal is inside a person, an object, or a place. **Sharing with others and caring for people are some of Zena's *internal* qualities.** *syn.* inner

ACADEMIC LANGUAGE

interview An *interview* is a series of questions and answers that give information about a topic or about the person being interviewed.

intonation *Intonation* is the rise and fall of your voice as you read aloud.

in·tri·cate [in′tri·kit] *adj.* If something is intricate, it is complicated or involved and has many small parts or details. **Psychologists try to understand the *intricate* reasons for certain behavior.** *syn.* complicated

in·va·sion [in·vā′zhən] *n.* An invasion happens when many people or animals enter a place all at once. **Sitting on the park bench, Elizabeth felt as if she were in the middle of an *invasion* of birds.** *syn.* intrusion

in·vest [in·vest′] *v.* To invest money in a project means that you put your funds into it, with the hope that in the future, it will earn more money. **Lester decided to *invest* in his uncle's successful business so that he, too, could earn a profit.** *syn.* finance

ir·re·pres·si·ble [ir·i·pres′ə·bəl] *adj.* A feeling or action that is irrepressible cannot be controlled or held back. **The scientist's *irrepressible* desire to explore nature led to his discovering a new species of ant.** *syns.* unmanageable, uncontainable

ir·re·sis·ti·ble [ir·i·zis′tə·bəl] *adj.* Something that is irresistible is difficult to turn away from. **Mother found the sparkling bracelet *irresistible*, so she bought it right away.** *syns.* appealing, desirable

a add	e end	o odd	o͞o pool	oi oil	th this
ā ace	ē equal	ō open	u up	ou pout	zh vision
â care	i it	ô order	û burn	ng ring	
ä palm	ī ice	o͝o took	yo͞o fuse	th thin	

ə = *a* in *above*, *e* in *sicken*, *i* in *possible*, *o* in *melon*, *u* in *circus*

i·so·lat·ed [ī′sə·lāt′əd] *adj.* A place that is isolated is a long way from large towns and is difficult to reach. **Sofia lives out in the countryside on an *isolated* farm.**
syn. secluded

isolated

jet·ti·son [jet′ə·sən] *v.* **jet·ti·soned** Something that is jettisoned is deliberately cast away from a moving object, sometimes to make the object lighter. **Before the boat sank, we *jettisoned* the extra cargo and paddled to shore.** *syn.* discard

Word Origins

jettison The word *jettison* can be traced to the Latin word *jectáre,* meaning "to toss about." Later, the French changed *jectáre* to *getaison* and used it to mean "the act of throwing (goods overboard)."

lad·en [lād′ən] *v.* If something is laden, it is weighed with a heavy load. **Sandra was *laden* with stacks of books to use for her research report.** *syn.* overloaded

ACADEMIC LANGUAGE

legend A *legend* is a story passed down through time and often reflects the beliefs or values of a culture. It may be based on real people or places.

loathe [lōth] *v.* If you loathe something, you hate it. **My friends *loathe* being asked to wear formal clothing to parties.**
syns. dislike, detest

ACADEMIC LANGUAGE

magazine article A *magazine article* gives information on a topic and usually includes photographs with captions.

ma·neu·ver [mə·n(y)o͞o′vər] *v.* **ma·neu·vered** To have maneuvered something is to have moved it or guided it very carefully. **The captain *maneuvered* the boat into its slip near the dock.**
syns. manipulate, manage

ma·ven [mā′vən] *n.* A maven is someone with special knowledge about a particular subject. **My science teacher is a *maven* on the subject of migrating birds.**
syn. expert

meas·ly [mēz′lē] *adj.* A measly amount of something is a very small amount. **Sherwin got a *measly* half-cup of soup with his sandwich.** *syns.* scanty, insufficient

men·tor [men′tər] *n.* A mentor is a trusted person who gives a person helpful advice. **Trina's volleyball *mentor* teaches excellent playing strategies that she learned while playing on a professional team.** *syn.* teacher

FACT FILE

mentor In Greek mythology, Mentor was a friend of Odysseus, the hero of Homer's epic poem *The Odyssey.* Mentor was the helper and teacher of Odysseus' son, Telemachus. After Odysseus went away to battle, Mentor often helped Telemachus choose the right course of action.

mis·treat [mis·trēt′] *v.* **mis·treat·ed** If something is mistreated, it is used in a way that harms or hurts it. **Sam thought his younger sister *mistreated* her bicycle by leaving it outside on the wet grass every evening.** *syn.* harm

mod·est [mod′əst] *adj.* A modest person does not brag or show off. **Hardly anyone knew that Sally had shown her paintings in several art galleries because she was *modest* about her talent.** *syn.* humble

mo·nop·o·lize [mə·nop′ə·līz] *v.* People who monopolize something control it and prevent others from using it. **Marcos tries not to *monopolize* the remote control when he watches TV with his friends.** *syn.* dominate

FACT FILE

monopolize *Monopolize* can be traced back to the Greek word *monopolion.* The word part *mono* means "single," and *polein* means "to sell." The popular board game *Monopoly,* in which players buy and sell property, appeared in 1935.

mo·not·o·nous [mə·not′ə·nəs] *adj.* If something is monotonous, it is repetitive and boring. **Juanita says that practicing the musical scales over and over on the piano is *monotonous.*** *syns.* boring, tedious

mor·ti·fy [môr′tə·fī] *v.* **mor·ti·fied** If you feel mortified, you feel extremely embarrassed or ashamed. **Shawna was *mortified* during the play when she couldn't remember her most important lines.** *syns.* humiliate, embarrass

ACADEMIC LANGUAGE

myth A *myth* is an imaginative story that explains how people and places came to be. Myths are often based on what a group of people in the past believed.

N

ACADEMIC LANGUAGE

narrative nonfiction *Narrative nonfiction* is a story that tells about people, things, events, or places that are real.

nudge [nuj] *v.* **nudged** If you nudged a person or thing, you pushed it or poked it gently. **I forgot to set my alarm clock last night, so it's a good thing my dog *nudged* me when it was time to get up.** *syn.* push

O

or·deal [ôr·dēl′ *or* ôr·dē′əl] *n.* An ordeal is a very difficult experience that is unpleasant to go through. **Living through the flood was an *ordeal*, but rebuilding our community was just as difficult.** *syn.* challenge

a	add	e	end	o	odd	o͞o	pool	oi	oil	th	this
ā	ace	ē	equal	ō	open	u	up	ou	pout	zh	vision
â	care	i	it	ô	order	û	burn	ng	ring		
ä	palm	ī	ice	o͝o	took	yo͞o	fuse	th	thin		

ə = *a* in *above*, *e* in *sicken*, *i* in *possible*, *o* in *melon*, *u* in *circus*

ACADEMIC LANGUAGE

organization Writers create *organization* by ordering ideas in ways that make sense, such as in a time-order sequence. Stories, poems, essays, and other genres are organized according to rules and patterns specific to each writing form.

out·cast [out′kast] *n.* An outcast is someone who has been rejected or driven out by others. **After Hannah became a theater star, she was an *outcast* among her old friends because she went for weeks without calling them.** *syn.* outsider

out·land·ish [out·lan′dish] *adj.* If something is outlandish, it is bizarre, strange, and unusual. **The clowns wore *outlandish* outfits, making everyone smile.** *syn.* peculiar

outlandish

o·ver·come [ō·vər·kum′] *v.* When you are overcome by something, you are overpowered by it. **Derek was *overcome* by a sudden fear of speaking in front of the group.** *syn.* overwhelm

P

ACADEMIC LANGUAGE

pace Reading aloud at an appropriate *pace* means reading with smoothness and consistency, not too fast or too slow.

pan·ic [pan′ik] *n.* Panic is a strong feeling of fear and anxiety that makes a person act unreasonably or without thinking carefully. **When the burglar alarm sounded, Jocelyn went into a state of *panic* and started to scream.** *syn.* fear

FACT FILE

panic The word *panic* comes from *Pānikós,* the Greek word that means "of Pan." In Greek mythology, Pan is the god of the woods. The Greek people believed that Pan startled animals in the woods and caused them to run or fly away.

parched [pärcht] *adj.* Something that is parched is dried out from lack of water. **The farmer hoped the rain clouds in the distance would bring much-needed water to his *parched* fields of corn.** *syn.* dehydrated

per·il [per′əl] *n.* Peril is great danger. **Claire visited the library during the day because walking alone at night would put her in *peril*.** *syns.* danger, risk

per·se·ver·ance [pûr·sə·vir′əns] *n.* If you try hard and don't give up, you are showing perseverance. **Margaret's many hours of practicing her gymnastics routine showed her *perseverance*.** *syn.* determination

ACADEMIC LANGUAGE

personal narrative In *personal narratives,* authors reveal thoughts and feelings about their experiences. Personal narratives are told in first-person point of view.

per·suade [pər·swād′] *v.* **per·suad·ing** Persuading someone means trying to get him or her to agree with your plan or opinion. **Richard was intent on *persuading* Fernando to play tennis with him.** *syn.* convince

ACADEMIC LANGUAGE

persuasive text *Persuasive text* is written to persuade readers to take action or to convince them of the author's viewpoint on a topic. Editorials, reviews, and advertisements are examples of persuasive text.

pes·ky [pes′kē] *adj.* Something that is pesky is annoying but not important. **Picnics are a lot of fun until those *pesky* ants show up!** *syns.* annoying, irritating

pho·bi·a [fō′bē·ə] *n.* To have a phobia is to be terrified of something without having a good reason for the fear. **Tyrell's *phobia* of flying kept him from traveling to faraway places.** *syn.* fear

ACADEMIC LANGUAGE

photo essay A *photo essay* gives information through photographs and captions.

phrasing *Phrasing* is grouping words into meaningful "chunks," or phrases, when you read aloud.

pin·na·cle [pin′ə·kəl] *n.* The pinnacle of a building is a tall, pointed piece at its top. **The *pinnacle* of the Empire State Building lights up at night.** *syns.* peak, top

pinnacle

ACADEMIC LANGUAGE

play A *play* is a story that is meant to be performed for an audience. Plays often include stage directions that tell the characters how to act and may be divided into acts and scenes.

poetry *Poetry* is a form of expressive writing that uses verse.

poised [poizd] *adj.* When you are poised, you are calm and ready to get started. **The ballerina stood *poised* in the wings, waiting for her cue.** *syn.* composed

a add	e end	o odd	o͞o pool	oi oil	th this	ə = *a* in *above*
ā ace	ē equal	ō open	u up	ou pout	zh vision	*e* in *sicken*
â care	i it	ô order	û burn	ng ring		*i* in *possible*
ä palm	ī ice	o͝o took	yo͞o fuse	th thin		*o* in *melon*
						u in *circus*

port·a·ble [pôr′tə·bəl] *adj.* Something that is portable can be moved or carried by hand. **We laughed because Dad brought a *portable* TV and his cell phone on the camping trip.** *syn.* movable

po·ten·tial·ly [pə·ten′chə·lē] *adv.* Something that could potentially happen could possibly happen. **If Ken studies more, he *potentially* could get all *A*'s.** *syn.* probably

prac·ti·cal [prak′ti·kəl] *adj.* Something that is practical is useful. **Even though the winter coat was on sale, Erin didn't think it would be *practical* for her summer vacation in Arizona.** *syns.* useful, realistic

Word Origins

practical The word *practical* came from the Greek word *praktikos,* which means "fit for action." It was used later in Middle English as *practicale*.

pre·car·i·ous [pri·kâr′ē·əs] *adj.* In a precarious situation, things are uncertain and can suddenly become dangerous. **Cheng didn't hear the lifeguard's warning and found himself in the *precarious* state of swimming in rough water.** *syns.* risky, uncertain

pre·cious [presh′əs] *adj.* If something is precious to you, it has value and special meaning to you. **Martha never misses appointments for her dog's check-ups because he is *precious* to her.** *syn.* valued

pres·ti·gious [pres·tē′jəs] *adj.* Something that is prestigious is highly respected and admired. **The principal of a school has a *prestigious* job.** *syns.* impressive, noteworthy

pro·claim [prō·klām′] *v.* **pro·claimed** If you have announced something to a group of people, you have proclaimed it. **The referee *proclaimed* to the crowd that the hometown team was the district winner.** *syns.* announce, declare

pro·fuse·ly [prō·fyo͞os′lē] *adv.* Something done profusely is done in great quantity. **Clifton apologized *profusely* after insulting his good friend.** *syns.* lavishly, exuberantly

prog·nos·ti·ca·tion [prog·nos′tə·kā′shən] *n.* A prognostication is a forecast or prediction. **After watching the football team of every school, the sports writer made a *prognostication* about which team would be the best that year.** *syn.* prediction

pro·por·tion [prə·pôr′shən] *n.* If something is in proportion, none of its parts are too large or too small. **The class's diorama of New York City showed the figures and automobiles in the correct *proportion* to the tall buildings.** *syns.* ratio, size

pro·pose [prə·pōz′] *v.* **pro·posed** A person who proposed something put forth the ideas to do it. **The best ideas for the fund-raiser were *proposed* by the new girl because she had ideas we had never thought of.** *syns.* suggest, recommend

pro·test [prō′test] *n.* A protest is a way of demonstrating that you are against something. **The parents held a *protest* about having too many soda machines and not enough water fountains in the school building.** *syn.* objection

pro·trude [prō·tro͞od′] *v.* To protrude is to stick out. **If the lumber will *protrude* from the back of the truck, you should tie a red cloth to the end of it so that other drivers can see it.** *syns.* jut, obtrude

pro·voke [prə·vōk′] *v.* When you provoke someone, you do something to make him or her feel angry. **Kathryn didn't mean to *provoke* Sol when she didn't return the CD she had borrowed.** *syns.* aggravate, irritate

pry [prī] *v.* **pried** If you have pried something off, you have forced it away from a surface. **A nail can usually be *pried* from a board by using the right tool.** *syn.* extract

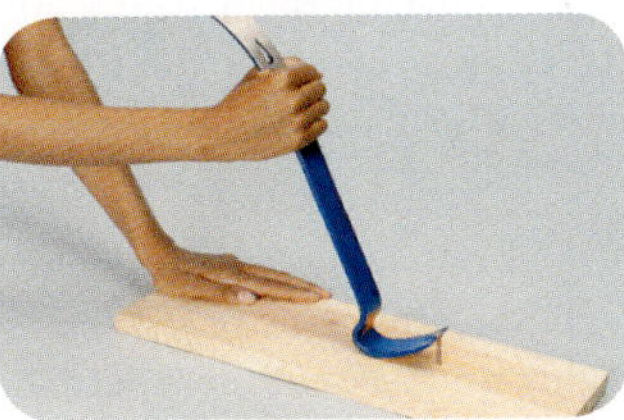

pry

R

rasp·y [ras′pē] *adj.* A raspy noise sounds rough and harsh, like sandpaper scraping wood. **Leon's voice sounded *raspy* because he had a chest cold.** *syns.* gruff, harsh

ACADEMIC LANGUAGE

reading rate Your *reading rate* is how quickly you can read a text correctly and still understand what you are reading.

realistic fiction *Realistic fiction* stories have characters, settings, and plot events that are like people, places, and events in real life. The characters face problems that could really happen.

re·coil [ri·koil′] *v.* To recoil means to jerk back suddenly. **The dog's loud barking made the cat *recoil* and run away.** *syn.* withdraw

re·count [ri·kount′] *v.* If you recount a story, you tell what happened. **Glendina's reading assignment was to *recount* the story in a summary.** *syn.* tell

re·gal [rē′gəl] *adj.* If something is regal, it is fit for a king or queen. **The German hotel looked *regal,* and we found out later that it had once been a real palace.** *syn.* majestic

reign [rān] *v.* **reigned** If someone has reigned, he or she has been very important in a particular place. **Principal Jones *reigned* over Southeast Middle School until he retired last June.** *syn.* preside

re·lent [ri·lent′] *v.* **re·lent·ed** Someone who has relented has agreed to something he or she once refused. **The students cheered when the school principal *relented* and allowed them to have a "bring-your-pet-to-school" day.** *syn.* yield

re·mote [ri·mōt′] *adj.* A remote place is far away from cities and towns. **Kyle's grandparents live in such a *remote* area that the only things they hear outside are the wind, the birds, and the insects.** *syns.* faraway, secluded

re·plen·ish [ri·plen′ish] *v.* **re·plen·ish·ing** Replenishing something means refilling it or making it complete again. **Next weekend, my parents will be going to the market and *replenishing* our refrigerator with food.** *syns.* refill, restock

rep·u·ta·tion [rep′yə·tā′shən] *n.* A person's reputation is what he or she is known for. **The senator has a *reputation* for being honest and fair, so many people in the government trust him.**

a add	e end	o odd	o͞o pool	oi oil	th this	ə = *a* in *above*
ā ace	ē equal	ō open	u up	ou pout	zh vision	*e* in *sicken*
â care	i it	ô order	û burn	ng ring		*i* in *possible*
ä palm	ī ice	o͝o took	yo͞o fuse	th thin		*o* in *melon*
						u in *circus*

res·i·dent [rez′ə·dənt] *n.* **res·i·dents** Residents are the people or animals that live in a place. **Alligators and snakes are *residents* of many swamps.** *syns.* inhabitant, dweller

re·sist [ri·zist′] *v.* **re·sist·ed** If a person or an object has resisted, that person or object was very difficult or impossible to change. **The painting *resisted* all of Barry's attempts to restore it to its original condition.** *syn.* oppose

re·strain [ri·strān′] *v.* If you restrain something, you hold it back or limit it. **To *restrain* the sheep from wandering too far, the rancher put up a fence.** *syn.* control

rev·el·er [rev′əl·ər] *n.* **rev·el·ers** Revelers are people who are having fun at a lively party or celebration. **Cinco de Mayo is a Mexican holiday in which *revelers* enjoy parades and parties.** *syn.* partygoer

rig·id [rij′id] *adj.* An object that is rigid is stiff and does not change shape easily. **When the clay hardens, the sculpture becomes *rigid*.** *syn.* firm

> **Word Origins**
>
> **rigid** The word *rigid* is based on the Latin word *rigere,* which means "to be stiff."

row·dy [rou′dē] *adj.* People who are rowdy are noisy, rough, and out of control. **Guards monitored the crowd of *rowdy* fans as they exited the rugby stadium.** *syn.* disorderly

ruck·us [ruk′əs] *n.* To raise a ruckus is to make a lot of noise and fuss about something. **The dog alerted its sleeping owner of danger by making a *ruckus*.** *syn.* disturbance

schol·ar [skol′ər] *n.* **schol·ars** Scholars are people who have studied certain topics and know a lot about them. **Many English professors are *scholars* in the literature of a particular time period.** *syn.* intellectual

scour [skour] *v.* **scours** If someone scours a place for something, he or she searches thoroughly for it. **Penelope *scours* the yard in hopes of finding her necklace.** *syn.* search

se·cure [si·kyŏŏr′] *adj.* Something that is secure is safe and not likely to give way. **Evelyn uses a *secure* lock on her door to keep out intruders.** *syns.* safe, protected

secure

> **Word Origins**
>
> **secure** The word *secure* came from the Latin phrase *se cura,* which means "free from care." The word was first used in English with its current meaning in about 1533.

sel·dom [sel′dəm] *adv.* If something seldom happens, it hardly ever happens. **Rainbows are *seldom* seen in desert areas.** *syns.* rarely, infrequently

sen·si·bil·i·ty [sen′sə·bil′ə·tē] *n.* A sensibility is a special awareness in a certain area; for example, a person can have an artistic sensibility or a musical sensibility. **The interior designer has a *sensibility* for creating a mood through the use of color.** *syn.* feeling

ACADEMIC LANGUAGE

sentence fluency Writers use a variety of *sentence* types and lengths to add interest to their writing. Simple, compound, and complex sentences are a few of the sentence types writers use.

shat·ter [shat′ər] *v.* When things shatter, they break suddenly and violently into small pieces. **If the puppies knock over the vase, it will *shatter* into a hundred pieces.** *syns.* break, destroy

sin·cere [sin·sir′] *adj.* If you are being sincere, you are being honest, and you mean what you say. **Joyce was *sincere* when she told the teacher she liked doing science experiments.** *syns.* honest, genuine

FACT FILE

sincere Most experts trace the word *sincere* to the Latin word *sincerus,* meaning "clean, pure, or sound." However, other experts say the word has its roots in the marble quarries of the sixteenth century, in which workers would rub wax on marble blocks to hide flaws. In time, the government declared that all marble had to be *sine cera,* or "without wax."

sleek [slēk] *adj.* Something that is sleek is smooth. **A seal's wet fur looks *sleek*.** *syns.* shiny, glossy

sleek

smirk [smûrk] *n.* A smirk is an unkind smile. **The producer had a *smirk* on his face as he talked about the famous actor having trouble finding work.** *syn.* simper

sneer [snir] *v.* **sneered** If you sneered at someone, you showed with your words and expression that you had little respect for that person. **The arrogant hotel guest *sneered* at the desk clerk when he couldn't find her reservation.** *syn.* scoff

som·ber·ly [som′bər·lē] *adv.* When you act somberly, you speak and act in a serious way. **The news anchor *somberly* reported the details of the train accident.** *syns.* seriously, sadly

sor·row·ful [sor′ə·fəl] *adj.* If you feel sorrowful, you are sad. **The listeners were *sorrowful* as they heard about the victims of the fire.** *syns.* distressed, unhappy

spe·cial·ize [spesh′əl·īz] *v.* **spe·cial·ized** Someone who has specialized in something has given it most of his or her time and attention. **The doctor *specialized* in heart surgery.** *syns.* concentrate, focus

a add	e end	o odd	o͞o pool	oi oil	th this	ə = *a* in *above*
ā ace	ē equal	ō open	u up	ou pout	zh vision	*e* in *sicken*
â care	i it	ô order	û burn	ng ring		*i* in *possible*
ä palm	ī ice	o͝o took	yo͞o fuse	th thin		*o* in *melon*
						u in *circus*

spec·i·men [spes′ə·mən] *n.* **spec·i·mens** Specimens are examples of things scientists collect in order to study. **Entomologists collect *specimens* of insects.** *syn.* sample

spec·tac·u·lar [spek·tak′yə·lər] *adj.* Something that is spectacular is very impressive and draws a lot of attention. **Lei's room faces west, giving her views of the region's *spectacular* sunsets.** *syn.* amazing

squint [skwint] *v.* **squint·ing** Someone who is squinting is squeezing his or her eyes partly shut in order to see. **It's hard to have a picture taken on a bright, sunny day without *squinting*.** *syn.* peer

stam·mer [stam′ər] *v.* **stam·mers** A person who stammers speaks with difficulty, often stopping or repeating himself or herself. **Because she is nervous, Ines *stammers* as she gives her speech.** *syn.* stutter

stream·lined [strēm′līnd] *adj.* A streamlined design is efficient and has no unneeded parts. **The car salesperson boasted about the *streamlined* design of the new, faster sports model.** *syn.* sleek

strick·en [strik′ən] *v.* If you are stricken, you are suddenly and badly affected by something, such as illness or fear. **When Stanley heard that the tornado had demolished all of the houses in his community, he was *stricken* with grief.** *syn.* afflict

sum·mit [sum′it] *n.* A mountain's summit is its very top. **While touring Kenya, Janeka climbed to the *summit* of Mt. Kilimanjaro.** *syns.* top, peak

Word Origins

summit The word *summit* has its origins in the Latin word *summus,* meaning "highest." When the French adopted the word *summus,* they changed it to *sommette,* meaning "the highest part or top of a hill."

sus·tain [sə·stān′] *v.* When you sustain something, you keep it going by giving it what it needs. **In order to *sustain* the school library, the parents donated money and books.** *syns.* maintain, continue

swarm [swôrm] *v.* **swarmed** If animals have swarmed, they have moved quickly and gathered in large numbers. **In the spring, honeybees *swarmed* around the nest to protect the queen bee.** *syns.* group, cluster

sway [swā] *v.* **swayed** Something that swayed was moving back and forth. **The audience *swayed* to the music of the orchestra.** *syn.* rock

T

ACADEMIC LANGUAGE

tall tale A *tall tale* is a humorous story about impossible or exaggerated happenings.

teem [tēm] *v.* **teem·ing** Something that is teeming is overflowing with life or energy. **The stadium was *teeming* with fans for the championship soccer game.** *syn.* abound

tempt [tempt] *v.* **tempt·ed** If you are tempted to do something, you really want to do it, even though you know you shouldn't. **Natalia is *tempted* to listen to her new CD instead of writing her book report.** *syn.* entice

ten·den·cy [ten′dən·sē] *n.* To have a tendency is to have a habit of doing something in a certain way. **Because Arup has a *tendency* to wait until the last minute to do his assignments, he often turns in his work late.** *syn.* inclination

ter·rain [tə·rān′] *n.* Terrain is the kind of land that is found in a place; for example, terrain might be rocky, hilly, or swampy. **Laticia enjoys hiking the rocky *terrain* in the state park.** *syns.* land, territory

terrain

Word Origins

terrain The word *terrain* can be traced back to the Latin word *terra*, meaning "earth." The word was later used by the French as *terrain*.

ACADEMIC LANGUAGE

textbook *Textbooks* are organized by chapter titles and headings within chapters. Textbooks provide information without giving the authors' opinions.

throng [throng] *n.* A throng is a crowd of people. **The shouts became louder as the *throng* waited for the doors to open.** *syns.* crowd, mass

ACADEMIC LANGUAGE

time line A *time line* shows information about events in the order in which they happened.

tran·quil·i·ty [trang·kwil′ə·tē] *n.* A feeling of tranquility is a feeling of calm and peace. **Jessica finds *tranquility* in sitting beside the pond and observing nature.** *syn.* serenity

tur·bu·lent [tûr′byə·lənt] *adj.* Something that is turbulent, such as air or water, has strong currents which change direction suddenly. **The captain of the airplane turned on the seat-belt sign and announced that the weather had become *turbulent*.** *syn.* unsettled

U

un·der·ly·ing [un′dər·lī′ing] *adj.* Something that is underlying is located below or beneath something. **An ant mound's underlying soil has a network of tunnels made and used by thousands of ants.**

un·fath·om·a·ble [un·fath′əm·ə·bəl] *adj.* If something is unfathomable, it cannot be understood or known. **Without an understanding of basic arithmetic, college algebra would be *unfathomable*.** *syn.* incomprehensible

un·im·ag·i·na·ble [un·i·maj′ə·nə·bəl] *adj.* If something is unimaginable, it is impossible to think that it might happen or exist. **A summer without sunshine is *unimaginable*.** *syns.* unthinkable, inconceivable

a add	e end	o odd	o͞o pool	oi oil	th̶ this	ə = *a* in *above*
ā ace	ē equal	ō open	u up	ou pout	zh vision	*e* in *sicken*
â care	i it	ô order	û burn	ng ring		*i* in *possible*
ä palm	ī ice	o͝o took	yo͞o fuse	th thin		*o* in *melon*
						u in *circus*

un·in·hab·it·a·ble [un·in·hab′it·ə·bəl] *adj.* A place that is uninhabitable cannot be lived in. **This place will be *uninhabitable* until the water can be made clean and safe to drink.** *syn.* inhospitable

ur·gent·ly [ûr′jənt·lē] *adv.* If you urgently tell someone to do something, it is important that it be done right away. **Phillip's father *urgently* needs him to help make all the deliveries before dark.** *syn.* immediately

V

van·ish [van′ish] *v.* To vanish is to disappear suddenly. **The magician made the tiger seem to *vanish* and then appear again.** *syn.* disappear

veto [vē′tō] *v.* **ve·toed** If someone has vetoed something, he or she has rejected it. **Congress passed the bill, but the President *vetoed* it.** *syn.* reject

FACT FILE

veto During government sessions in ancient Rome, elected members, called tribunes, yelled "*Veto!*" if they did not want a law to pass. *Veto* is Latin for "I forbid."

vi·tal [vīt′əl] *adj.* Something that is vital is necessary for life. **Food, air, and water are *vital* for survival.** *syn.* essential

ACADEMIC LANGUAGE

voice The term *voice* is used to describe a writer's tone, attitude, or personality. A reader might perceive a writer's voice as formal, confident, or mischievous.

W

wisp·y [wisp′ē] *adj.* Something that is wispy is thin, lightweight, and easily broken. **Rosa's china doll was so fragile and *wispy* that she was afraid to play with it.** *syn.* delicate

wist·ful [wist′fəl] *adj.* You are wistful if you feel as though your wishes probably won't come true. **Sheila felt *wistful* knowing she wouldn't be going to music camp this summer.** *syn.* melancholy

with·ered [wi*th*′ərd] *adj.* Something that is withered is dried up and faded. **The fallen leaves were brown and *withered*.** *syn.* wilted

withered

ACADEMIC LANGUAGE

word choice A writer may choose sensory, vivid, and precise words to help the reader imagine people, places, and events. *Word choice* helps writers express a personal voice, or personality, in their writing.

Y

yearn·ing [yûr′ning] *n.* A yearning is a great desire to have something that you may never be able to get. **Gracie has a *yearning* to travel to the Amazon rain forest to see the many flowers that she has only read about.** *syns.* desire, longing

Acknowledgments

For permission to reprint copyrighted material, grateful acknowledgment is made to the following sources:

Atheneum Books for Young Readers, an imprint of Simon & Schuster Children's Publishing Division: From *Ultimate Field Trip 3: Wading into Marine Biology* by Susan E. Goodman, photographs by Michael J. Doolittle. Text copyright © 1999 by Susan E. Goodman; photographs copyright © 1999 by Michael J. Doolittle.

Curtis Brown, Ltd.: "Summer Hummers" by Linda Sue Park. Text copyright © 2001 by Linda Sue Park. Originally published in *Cricket* Magazine, November 2001 by Carus Publishing Company.

Candlewick Press, Inc., Cambridge, MA: From *Interrupted Journey* by Kathryn Lasky, photographs by Christopher G. Knight. Text copyright © 2001 by Kathryn Lasky; photographs copyright © 2001 by Christopher G. Knight.

Carus Publishing Company, 30 Grove St., Suite C, Peterborough, NH 03458: "Got a Problem? Get a Plan!" by Karen Bledsoe from *APPLESEEDS: Kids Can Change the World,* September 2005. Text © 2005 by Carus Publishing Company. "Central Park" by John J. Bonk from *COBBLESTONE: New York City,* June 1995. Text © 1995 by Cobblestone Publishing. "Voyage into the Past" by Ann Collins from *APPLESEEDS: American Places, San Diego,* May 2000. Text © 2000 by Cobblestone Publishing. "Journey on the Silk Road" by Luann Hankom from *APPLESEEDS: Children of China Long Ago,* October 2002. Text © 2002 by Carus Publishing Company. "Sourdough" by Jane Scherer from *COBBLESTONE: The California Gold Rush,* December 1997. Text © 1997 by Cobblestone Publishing.

Children's Press, an imprint of Scholastic Library Publishing, Inc.: From *Lewis and Clark* by R. Conrad Stein. Text © 1997 by Children's Press®, a division of Grolier Publishing Co., Inc.

Chronicle Books LLC, San Francisco, ChronicleBooks.com: From *The Man Who Went to the Far Side of the Moon: The Story of Apollo 11 Astronaut Michael Collins* by Bea Uusma Schyffert. Text and illustrations copyright © 1999 by Bea Uusma Schyffert; translation © 2003 by Chronicle Books LLC.

Clarion Books, a Houghton Mifflin Company imprint: From *Project Mulberry* by Linda Sue Park, cover illustration by Debora Smith. Text copyright © 2005 by Linda Sue Park; cover illustration copyright © 2005 by Debora Smith.

The Cricket Magazine Group, a division of Carus Publishing Company: "Ninth Inning" by Anna Levine from *Cricket* Magazine, June 2004. Text © 2004 by Anna Levine. "Take a Bow!" by Anna Levine from *Cricket* Magazine, January 2005. Text © 2004 by Anna Levine.

Darby Creek Publishing, a division of Oxford Resources, Inc.: "Line Drive" by Tanya West Dean from *Sport Shorts: An Anthology of Short Stories.* Text © 2005 by Tanya West.

Dial Books for Young Readers, a Division of Penguin Young Readers Group, A Member of Penguin Group (USA) Inc., 345 Hudson Street, New York, NY 10014: "On Top of the World" from *A World of Wonders: Geographic Travels in Verse and Rhyme* by J. Patrick Lewis, illustrated by Alison Jay. Text copyright © 2002 by J. Patrick Lewis; illustration copyright © 2002 by Alison Jay.

Farrar, Straus and Giroux, LLC: From *Chang and the Bamboo Flute* by Elizabeth Starr Hill, cover illustration by Lesley Liu. Text copyright © 2002 by Elizabeth Starr Hill; cover illustration copyright © 2002 by Lesley Liu. From *Chester Cricket's Pigeon Ride* by George Selden, illustrated by Garth Williams. Text copyright © 1981 by George Selden Thompson; illustrations copyright © 1981 by Garth Williams.

HarperCollins Publishers: From *When the Circus Came to Town* by Laurence Yep, cover illustration by Suling Wang. Text copyright © 2002 by Laurence Yep; cover illustration copyright © 2002 by Suling Wang.

Highlights for Children, Inc., Columbus, OH: "When Our Family Bands Together" by Teresa Bateman from *Highlights for Children* Magazine, August 2003. Text copyright © 2003 by Highlights for Children, Inc. "The Alligator Race" by Karen Dowicz Haas from *Highlights for Children* Magazine, August 2004. Text copyright © 2004 by Highlights for Children, Inc. From "The Artist's Eye" by Joan T. Zeier in *Highlights for Children* Magazine, March 2004. Text copyright © 2004 by Highlights for Children, Inc.

Houghton Mifflin Company: "Steam" from *Splish Splash* by Joan Bransfield Graham. Text copyright © 1994 by Joan Bransfield Graham. From *The Top of the World: Climbing Mount Everest* by Steve Jenkins. Copyright © 1999 by Steve Jenkins.

Alfred A. Knopf, an imprint of Random House Children's Books, a division of Random House, Inc.: From *The Daring Nellie Bly: America's Star Reporter* by Bonnie Christensen. Copyright © 2003 by Bonnie Christensen. "Stormalong" from *American Tall Tales* by Mary Pope Osborne. Text copyright © 1991 by Mary Pope Osborne. From "How Beaver Stole Fire" in *In a Circle Long Ago* by Nancy Van Laan, illustrated by Lisa Desimini. Text copyright © 1995 by Nancy Van Laan; illustrations copyright © 1995 by Lisa Desimini.

Lerner Publications Company: From *Nellie Bly's Book: Around the World in 72 Days* (Retitled: "A Proposal to Girdle the Earth"), edited by Ira Peck. Text copyright © 1998 by Ira Peck. *Little, Brown and Co., Inc.:* From *Into a New Country: Eight Remarkable Women of the West* (Retitled: "Klondike Kate") by Liza Ketchum. Text copyright © 2000 by Liza Ketchum.

Mary Anne Lloyd: Illustrations by Mary Anne Lloyd from "Kids in Action" by Elizabeth Schleichert in *Ranger Rick®* Magazine, September 2005.

Gina Maccoby Literary Agency: "Ice Cycle" by Mary Ann Hoberman from *Once Upon Ice,* selected by Jane Yolen. Text copyright © 1997 by Mary Ann Hoberman. Published by Boyds Mills Press, Inc.

National Geographic Society: From "The Zoo Crew" by Laura Daily in *National Geographic WORLD* Magazine, February 2000. Text copyright © 2000 by National Geographic Society. From *Inventing the Future* by Marfé Ferguson Delano. Text copyright © 2002 by National Geographic Society.

National Wildlife Federation®: From "Kids In Action" by Elizabeth Schleichert in *Ranger Rick®* Magazine, September 2005. Text copyright 2005 by the National Wildlife Federation®.

North-South Books Inc., New York: Sailing Home: A Story of a Childhood at Sea by Gloria Rand, illustrated by Ted Rand. Text copyright © 2001 by Gloria Rand; illustrations copyright © 2001 by Ted Rand.

G. P. Putnam's Sons, A Division of Penguin Young Readers Group, A Member of Penguin Group USA (Inc.), 345 Hudson Street, New York, NY 10014: From *Leonardo's Horse* by Jean Fritz, illustrated by Hudson Talbott. Text copyright © 2001 by Jean Fritz; illustrations copyright © 2001 by Hudson Talbott.

Marian Reiner, on behalf of August House Publishers, Inc.: "Paul Bunyan Makes Progress" from *Sweet Land of Story: Thirty-Six American Tales to Tell* by Pleasant deSpain. Text © 2000 by Pleasant deSpain. Published by August House Publishers, Inc.

Scholastic Inc.: "The Night of San Juan" and cover illustration from *Salsa Stories* by Lulu Delacre. Text and cover illustration copyright © 2000 by Lulu Delacre. From *Any Small Goodness: A Novel of the Barrio* by Tony Johnston, cover illustration by Raúl Colón. Text copyright © 2001 by Roger D. Johnston and Susan T. Johnston as Trustees of the Johnston Family Trust; cover illustration copyright © 2001 by Raúl Colón. Published by The Blue Sky Press. "Rain, Dance!" from *Splash! Poems of Our Watery World* by Constance Levy. Text copyright © 2002 by Constance Kling Levy. Published by Orchard Books. From *In 1776* by Jean Marzollo. Text copyright © 1994 by Jean Marzollo. "The Ant and the Dove," "The Lion and the Mouse," and cover illustration from *Aesop's Fables,* retold by Ann McGovern. Text and cover illustration copyright © 1963 by Scholastic Inc. Published by Apple Classics. *Nothing Ever Happens on 90th Street* by Roni Schotter, illustrated by Kyrsten Brooker. Text copyright © 1997 by Roni Schotter; illustrations copyright © 1997 by Kyrsten Brooker. Published by Orchard Books. From *A Drop of Water* by Walter Wick. Text and photographs copyright © 1997 by Walter Wick. Published by Scholastic Press.

Brian Selznick: Cover illustration by Brian Selznick from *The School Story* by Andrew Clements. Illustration copyright © 2001 by Brian Selznick.

Simon & Schuster Books for Young Readers, an Imprint of Simon & Schuster Children's Publishing Division: When Washington Crossed the Delaware by Lynne Cheney, illustrated by Peter M. Fiore. Text copyright © 2004 by Lynne Cheney; illustrations copyright © 2004 by Peter M. Fiore. From *The School Story* by Andrew Clements. Text copyright © 2001 by Andrew Clements.

TIME For Kids: "Tree Houses for Everyone" by Tiffany Sommers from *TIME For Kids* Magazine, September 24, 2004. From "Evren Ozan, Musician" by Harsha Viswanathan in *TIME For Kids* Magazine, October 27, 2003.

Albert Whitman & Company: From *Rope Burn* by Jan Siebold, cover illustration by Layne Johnson. Text copyright © 1998 by Jan Siebold; cover illustration © 1998 by Layne Johnson.

Photo Credits

Placement Key: (t) top, (b) bottom, (l) left, (r) right, (c) center 3 (br) ©Colibri/JupiterImages; 3 (tcr) Victoria Bowen/Harcourt; 4 (bl) ©Wolfgang Deuter/zefa/Corbis; 6 (bc) ©Bettman/CORBIS; 7 (cl) ©Michael S. Yamashita/COBIS; 7 (c) ©Tobias Titz/fStop/Getty Images; 16 (bl) ©Hulton-Deutsch Collection/Corbis; 22 (bl) ©Rob Melnychuk/Photodisc Red/Getty Images; 23 (cr) ©Ellen Rooney/Robert Harding World Imagery/Corbis; 25 (br) ©Envision/Corbis; 26 (bl) ©Randy Faris/CORBIS; 27 (cr) ©James Nazz/Corbis; 28 (b) ©Katja Zimmermann/Taxi/Getty Images; 33 (br) ©image100/Corbis; 35 (bc) ©Andrew Bordwin/Beateworks/Corbis; 35 (b) ©Carlos Dominguez/CORBIS; 44 (bc) ©David Frazier/Stone/Getty images; 47 (br) ©DK Limited/Corbis; 48 (inset) ©Paul Edmondson/CORBIS; 49 (br) ©Adam Gault/Digital Vision/Getty Images; 51 (br) ©Jules Frazier/Photodisc Green/Getty Images; 52 (inset) ©Michael Boys/CORBIS; 55 (br) ©Terry W. Eggers/CORBIS; 55 (bl) ©Royalty-Free/Corbis; 59 (cr) ©Don Mason/CORBIS; 59 (br) ©Harry Spurling/Corbis; 70 (bl) ©Treat Davidson; Frank Lane Picture Agency/CORBIS; 71 (tcr) ©dk / Alamy; 71 (br) ©Don Farral/Photodisc Red/Getty Images; 72 (bl) ©2006 Jupiterimages Corporation; 75 (bl) ©Digital Vision/Digital Vision/Getty Images; 75 (bc) ©Royalty-Free/Corbis; 76 (b) ©2006 Jupiterimages corporation; 76 (cr) ©Gary Withey/Bruce Coleman USA; 76 ©Joseph Wright of Derby/The Bridgeman Art Library/Getty Images; 79 (cl) ©Steve Bonini/The Image Bank/Getty Images; 82 (bl) ©Altrendo Images/Altrendo/Getty Images; 87 (c) ©Bob Thomas/Stone/Getty Images; 91 (cl) ©Maximilian Stock Ltd/photocuisine/Corbis; 91 (br) ©Jacqui Hurst/CORBIS; 95 (br) ©Raymond Gehman/ Corbis; 95 (tr) ©Royalty-Free/Corbis; 99 (bl) ©Chuck Savage/ Corbis; 111 (cl) ©David Michael Zimmerman/ Corbis; 118 (b) ©Simon Marcus/ Corbis; vi (b) © Patrick Blake / Alamy; vii (b) ©David Muench / Corbis.

All other photos from Harcourt School Photo Library and Photographers.

Illustration Credits

Cover Art: Laura and Eric Ovresat, Artlab, Inc.